Neighborhood Hope Dealerz

A guide to empower communities from within

By Mack Graham

Copyright Page

Dedication

To my late sister Shalanda - a brilliant mind who inspired me to write this book. Your intelligence, your compassion, and your tenacity in the face of adversity continue to motivate me every day. I hope this book can honor your legacy by inspiring others to create positive change in their communities.

To my daughter Layla - my reason for striving to create a better world. I want you to grow up in a world where you can chase your dreams without any systemic barriers holding you back. This book is dedicated to you, and to all the young people who deserve a fair and just society. I hope this book can help pave the way towards a brighter future for generations to come.

To my parents and older sister - the foundation of my support and love. Your unwavering encouragement and guidance have been essential to my personal and professional growth. This book is dedicated to you - the people who have always been there for me through the ups and downs. Thank you for inspiring me to pursue my passions and for showing me the importance of making a positive impact on the world.

Mack Graham

Table of Contents

Mack Graham

Mack Graham

Breaking The Cycle:
Empowering Our Communities As Hope Dealerz

What comes to mind when you hear the phrase "dope dealer"?

Dope dealers are often a manifestation of systemic oppression and poverty in our communities. Despite the illegal and dangerous nature of their activities, they are sometimes viewed as sources of inspiration and role models due to their perceived wealth and status. But it is crucial to understand the larger forces that drive these individuals towards this path, such as a lack of economic opportunities, inadequate education and healthcare systems, and persistent poverty.

It is a heart-wrenching reality that these individuals, who often struggle to survive, are forced to choose illegal activities to provide for themselves and their families. The allure of temporary financial relief and a sense of community can be irresistible, but addressing the root causes perpetuating this vicious cycle is essential. The impact of policing disproportionately targets our communities, only exacerbates the problem and fails to address the underlying issues.

However, there is hope. We, as hope dealers, have the potential to redirect our resources and energy towards addressing these root causes, becoming agents of progress and positive change in our communities. Such opportunities can include investing in job training programs, supporting education initiatives, and community development projects - we can break the cycle of poverty, violence, and crime, and empower those around us to do the same.

It's time for us to take concrete action and work towards creating a world that is truly just and equitable for all. While some progress has been made in recent years, it is not nearly enough. In 2020 and 2021, we witnessed a powerful moment where fiscal support for BIPOC-led organizations and those focused on racial justice spiked. However, this momentum did not last and unfortunately, in 2022, there was a decrease in support for these organizations.

According to the Nonprofit Finance Fund's 2022 State of the Nonprofit Sector Survey, there are deep-seated racial disparities in nonprofit experiences and funding levels. BIPOC-led nonprofits faced more service demand than white-led organizations, yet funding increases were not equally felt. Black-led organizations did not receive as much additional funding as other organizations. Furthermore, BIPOC-led organizations experienced less flexibility from foundation funders and greater funding restrictions than white-led nonprofits, continuing a longstanding discriminatory trend in nonprofit funding.

It's disheartening to see that the world seems more interested in performative gestures on social media than making real investments towards creating lasting change. However, we must not let this deter us from continuing to fight for a better future. "Neighborhood Hope Dealerz" is a powerful call to action, urging individuals, organizations, and governments to invest in community-led initiatives that promote health, well-being, and justice. This book is about taking action and creating tangible change. It is about empowering communities to become self-sufficient while also acknowledging and addressing the systemic issues that hold them back.

The book dives deep into the root causes of systemic oppression and the impact of policing and criminal justice practices on our communities. But it doesn't stop there - it also provides a path forward by highlighting the importance of funding community-led solutions, action items, and resources. The ultimate goal is to empower our communities and equip readers with the knowledge and understanding necessary to create a more just and equitable world.

This book is more than just a call to action. It's a spark of empowerment that has the power to break the cycle of poverty, violence, and crime. By working together and investing in community-led initiatives, we can create a world that is more just and equitable for all. "Neighborhood Hope Dealerz" is the first step towards that goal.

Embark with me on an illuminating journey as we delve into the persistent struggles faced by our communities. From the intersection of policing and systematic oppression to the power of community-led solutions, we'll uncover a rich tapestry of insights through research, analysis, and personal narratives. Join me in building a compelling case for sustained efforts to uplift and empower these communities.

Recognizing our role in spreading optimism and fostering good change is essential. Each of us may make a difference by lending our support to community-led projects, lending our time to worthy causes, or lobbying for policy reform. We can create a world where everyone can grow and attain their full potential if we raise awareness of the problems and work towards finding solutions.

Are you ready?

CHAPTER 1

<u>Uncovering the Truth:</u>

The Legacy Of Racism & Violence In American Policing & The Path To Reform

"In the era of mass incarceration, policing has become the central mechanism for producing and maintaining racial hierarchy in the United States." - Angela Davis

Growing up as a black man in New York City, I have been a firsthand witness to the systemic racism that pervades the NYPD. The memories of innocent black victims, like Abner Louima, who was brutalized by the police in 1997, Amadou Diallo, who was shot 41 times in 1999, and Sean Bell, who was shot 50 times, all unarmed and the officers responsible never facing the consequences, still haunt me to this day. In the case of Abner Louima, he was beaten and sexually assaulted with a broomstick by police officers in a bathroom of a Brooklyn precinct, leaving him with permanent physical and psychological scars. Amadou Diallo, a West African immigrant, was shot 41 times by four police officers who mistook his wallet for a gun. Sean Bell was killed just hours before his wedding, in a hail of 50 bullets, by police officers who claimed they thought he had a weapon. These are just a few examples of the countless instances of police brutality against black people in the United States, with too many more victims never seeing justice served.

Just a few blocks from my home, I saw Eric Garner's life taken by a police chokehold in 2014, and once again, justice was not served. The video of his death, with him gasping for air and saying, "I can't breathe," sparked nationwide protests and further highlighted the systemic problem of police brutality against black people.

By the time I was in high school, being stopped by the police had become a normal occurrence in my life. I grew up in the stop-and-frisk era, where people of color were disproportionately targeted and subjected to temporary detainment, questioning, and searches without cause. In 2011, the New York Police Department conducted over 684,000 stop and frisks, with over 87% of those stopped being black or Latino, despite only making up around 54% of the population in the city. This heightened tension between my community and the police left us little to no trust in law enforcement.

Driving while black is another form of racial profiling that has affected the lives of many black people, including myself. Despite having done nothing wrong, black drivers are often pulled over by the police for arbitrary reasons, such as, "driving while black". This practice has caused black people to experience a constant sense of fear and harassment while on the road, making driving a source of anxiety rather than a means of transportation.

From Slave Patrols to Public Safety The Legacy of US Policing and Systemic Oppression Against People of Color

1704	The first slave patrol is created in South Carolina to capture and punish runaway slaves, setting the foundation for modern-day policing.
1865	After the Civil War, the 13th Amendment abolishes slavery, but the Black Codes and Jim Crow laws are implemented, creating a new system of racial control that relies on policing and mass incarceration.
1893	The first state police force is established in Pennsylvania, and other states soon follow, increasing the power and reach of law enforcement.
1905	The first juvenile court is established in Cook County, Illinois, creating a new system of criminalizing youth and funneling them into the criminal justice system.
1920s-1930s	The Prohibition era leads to the rise of organized crime and the creation of the Federal Bureau of Investigation (FBI) to combat it, expanding the powers of law enforcement agencies.
1960s	The Civil Rights Movement and protests against the Vietnam War lead to clashes between police and demonstrators, and the militarization of police begins, with the government providing surplus military equipment to police departments.
1980s	The War on Drugs is declared, leading to a sharp increase in drug-related arrests and the growth of the prison-industrial complex.
1992	The Rodney King beating and subsequent riots in Los Angeles highlight police brutality and racism, leading to calls for police reform and community policing.
2001	The September 11 attacks lead to a focus on national security and counterterrorism, further increasing the power of law enforcement agencies and their ability to surveil and monitor citizens.
2020	The murder of George Floyd by Minneapolis police officers sparks protests and a nationwide reckoning with police brutality and systemic racism, leading to renewed calls for police reform and a reimagining of public safety.

Mack Graham

Despite all of this, my father, an NYPD officer, remains my greatest role model. He showed me that not all police officers are racist, and I knew he was still a black man, just like me, at the end of the day. However, systemic racism within law enforcement cannot be ignored. It is up to all of us to work towards creating a more equitable and just society where black people can feel safe and protected, both on the streets and in their interactions with the police.

It wasn't until I took an Africana Studies class in college that I realized the extent of the problem with policing and the history of discrimination against black people. The reality of systemic racism in the police force is a much larger issue that goes beyond just a few racist individuals in law enforcement. It is rooted in centuries of oppression and institutionalized racism. It will take a concerted effort from all of us to dismantle it and create a more just society for all.

The history of policing in America is a tale of bloodshed, racial inequality, and oppressive violence. Since its inception, communities of color have been targeted and subjected to brutal treatment by those who were supposed to keep the peace. The first police departments in the United States were established in the 19th century, modeled after British police forces. They were primarily focused on controlling crime and maintaining order through the use of force.

One of the most reprehensible examples of police brutality in American history is the establishment of slave patrols. These were groups of armed men in the antebellum South whose sole purpose was to track down and return escaped slaves to their owners. The slave patrols set a precedent for violence to maintain social order, particularly against communities of color, laying the foundation for modern policing. This legacy of violence and racial oppression still haunts policing practices today.

Mack Graham

The American policing system is built on a foundation of systemic racism and discrimination, disproportionately impacting communities of color. This is perpetuated through racial profiling, the over-policing of these communities, and excessive use of force. The issue of police brutality and racial profiling has been persistent throughout the history of policing in the United States, despite moments of progress and ongoing reforms.

Recent protests against police brutality and the call for systemic change reflect the growing desire to address the historical legacies of racism and violence in policing and create a fairer system. Addressing the troubled history of policing and its impact on communities of color is crucial for creating a brighter future for all.

Furthermore, it's imperative to examine the impact of police funding on our communities. Police funding often comes at the expense of community programs and initiatives that support education, health, and social services, particularly affecting communities of color who already face systemic barriers to accessing resources.

A concerning aspect of police budgets is allocating funds to pay settlements in police brutality cases. This sends a message that police departments view these settlements as a cost of doing business, shifting the burden to taxpayers. This financial incentive discourages departments from investing in reforms and training to prevent police brutality and improve community relations.

The history of policing in the United States is stained with violence, racial oppression, and neglect towards Our communities. To create a more just and equitable system, we must confront the historical legacies of racism and violence in policing, prioritize investments in community programs and initiatives, and re-evaluate the allocation of police funding. It's time to heal the wounds of the past and work towards a better future for all.

Mack Graham

Challenge:
Take action now to address the legacy of
racism and violence in American policing.
Sign an online petition calling for change.
Your signature can help show your support
for meaningful police reform and help
build momentum for change. With just a
few clicks, you can make a difference. Sign
a petition today and be a part of the
solution.

CHAPTER 2

Resurrecting a Legacy:
Learning from the Black Freedman's Savings & Trust Company to Achieve Financial Empowerment and Justice

"Until there is an actual economic and political equality for all, there will be neither peace nor justice." – Dr. Martin Luther King Jr.

African Americans have long been at the forefront of resilience, innovation, and creativity. Despite the many obstacles and challenges we have faced as a community; we have consistently proven that we can overcome and turn even the most difficult of circumstances into something truly remarkable. Our contributions to society have been nothing short of extraordinary, shaping not just our nation but the whole world.

However, despite our remarkable achievements, we have also been subjected to centuries of systemic oppression that has worked to keep us down, limit our opportunities, and manipulate our thoughts and beliefs. This has had a profound and lasting impact on our communities, shaping not only our experiences, but also our attitudes and beliefs about ourselves.

Growing up in Brooklyn, and later Staten Island, I was witness to this stark contrast between different communities. As a child, I observed the differences between the schools, the supermarkets, and the overall state of the neighborhood. I saw how crime, homelessness, poverty, and unemployment were much higher in the predominantly black areas, and how many people sought to escape these conditions by moving to whiter neighborhoods where they believed they would have access to better resources and opportunities.

As I got older, I came to understand the devastating impact of these systemic forces on our communities, and the need for us to work together to address and overcome them. The broken window theory, for example, highlights how poverty, neglect, and disinvestment in our communities can lead to a self-perpetuating cycle of decline. It is a cycle that can only be broken when we actively work to challenge the systems of oppression that created it and come together to build a better, more equitable, future for ourselves and our communities.

This task of overcoming the legacy of oppression and inequality will not be a simple feat. Still, it is one that must be pursued in order to bring about a brighter future for generations to come. The effort may be challenging, but the reward of unlocking the full potential of our community makes it a journey well worth taking. We must come together, make their voices heard, and actively work towards creating positive change.

The Black Freedman's Savings and Trust Company was more than just a financial institution. It was a symbol of hope, a beacon of light in the darkness of systemic oppression and racism that the African American community had faced for centuries. It offered the promise of a better future, where Black people could achieve financial stability, independence, and prosperity. The bank was established in

$24,100	$36,050	$189,100
Median wealth of Black families in 2019	Median wealth of Latinx families in 2019	Median wealth of White families in 2019

Source: Board of Governors of the Federal Reserve System, 2020 Survey of Consumer Finances

1865, in the aftermath of slavery and the American Civil War, with the goal of aiding newly freed slaves in their journey towards citizenship.

For many Black people, the Black Freedman's Savings and Trust Company was a source of pride and a source of strength. Through its services, the bank sought to counteract the effects of slavery and discrimination, and promote equality and justice for the Black community in the United States. It challenged the false notion that Black people were financially irresponsible and showed that they were capable of building wealth and achieving financial stability. It gave Black people a sense of ownership and control over their financial lives, something that had been denied to them for centuries.

The bank grew over the years and opened branches in major cities nationwide. It offered various financial services, including savings accounts and loans, to help Black people build wealth and stability. It also provided a sense of community and mutual support. People trusted the bank with their hard-earned savings, knowing their money was safe and secure. The bank was a source of empowerment and a pathway to a better future for Black people.

However, this dream was shattered when the Black Freedman's Savings and Trust Company failed in the late 19th century. Despite its noble goals and initial success, the bank was not able to withstand the economic turbulence of the times, including the Panic of 1873 and a depression that followed. The failure was a devastating blow to the African American community, and many depositors lost their savings. It was a loss that was felt deeply and personally, as it represented not just a loss of money but a loss of hope and trust.

The failure of the Black Freedman's Savings and Trust Company contributed to the limited access to financial services that Black people faced for many decades. It had a lasting impact on the African American community's ability to build wealth and achieve financial stability. The bank's failure was a reminder of the systemic barriers that continue to plague our communities from progressing toward economic parity and security.

The legacy of the Black Freedman's Savings and Trust Company is a reminder of the ongoing struggles faced by our communities in their pursuit of fiscal security and wealth. It is a call to action, a reminder that true justice and equity must be actively sought and won. The bank's failure is not just a story of what could have been, but a story of what must be. It is a story of hope, determination, resilience, and strength in the face of adversity. It is a story of the importance of community, mutual support and working towards a better future for all.

Today, we must continue to work towards a more just and equitable society, where all people have access to basic financial services and support. We must recommit ourselves to empowering our communities and building a future where everyone has the opportunity to achieve financial stability and prosperity. The legacy of the Black Freedman's Savings and Trust Company is a reminder of what can be achieved when we work together and a call to action to continue this work for generations to come.

Challenge:
Take control of your financial future and join the movement for financial empowerment and equity. Start by educating yourself about financial literacy and resources available to you. You can start by following accounts on social media, reading articles, attending workshops or webinars, or reaching out to organizations that support financial literacy and empowerment. Take the first step towards financial stability and security today and start learning about your options.

CHAPTER 3

Investing in Community Empowerment:

The Power of Funding Nonprofit Organizations and Community-Based Programs to Drive Lasting Change

"The measure of a society's greatness is its ability to produce, protect, and empower its people to achieve their potential." - Nelson Mandela

In 2020, I took on the challenge of becoming the executive director of the Long Beach Martin Luther King Center. This historic and significant organization was founded in 1967 by local black community organizers with the goal of serving Long Beach's children and families. The center has always been a symbol of black efforts to establish a community center that met the community's needs and combated systemic racism. Over the years, it has been an integral part of community activism and has played a critical role in the lives of not just African Americans, but also Caribbean-American, Central American, and Hispanic immigrants who have settled in the North Park community.

I was inspired by the organization's mission of "maintaining and improving the well-being of youth, adults, and seniors," and its commitment to revamping its service delivery systems by focusing on family strengths and working in partnership with families, schools, and other community-based organizations. But when I arrived, I was heartbroken to see the dire need for resources and support the organization faced. The COVID-19 pandemic only exacerbated the challenges, as the center became an essential first responder to the socio-economic difficulties faced by the African American and Latino children and families in the North Park Community.

The lack of funding and support for nonprofit organizations in our communities is a long-standing issue, and it was evident in the case of the Long Beach Martin Luther King Center. The organization struggled to attract staff in key roles due to salaries that were not competitive enough, leading to high turnover rates. This, in turn, made it difficult for the organization to focus on developing a structure to become financially sustainable. Instead, it was often reactive, putting out fires and missing the mark in providing the necessary services to make a sustainable change.

The importance of investing in community empowerment and funding nonprofit organizations and community-based programs cannot be overstated. These organizations play a critical role in addressing social issues and providing essential services to our communities that are often neglected by mainstream institutions.

Investing in community-based programs and nonprofit organizations is not just an act of generosity; it is a crucial investment in the future of our society. These organizations play a vital role in promoting health, well-being, and socio-economic growth, by providing essential resources, support, and advocacy to individuals and families in need. When they receive the necessary funding and resources, they can create a lasting impact that helps break the cycle of poverty, inequality, and social injustice, paving the way for a more equitable and just world for all. Despite the immense positive impact that these organizations can have, it is unfortunate that some may still fail to receive the support they need, leading to their eventual dissolution, like the Homeless Children's Education Fund.

The Homeless Children's Education Fund was a shining beacon of hope for homeless children in the Pittsburgh, Pennsylvania area. For many years, this community-based program provided vital educational support, resources, and advocacy for children who were struggling to make it through school while facing the challenges of homelessness.

The organization offered a wide range of services, including tutoring, school supplies, and enrichment programs, all designed to help homeless children stay in school and succeed academically. The goal was to give these children the tools they needed to overcome the obstacles they faced and achieve their full potential.

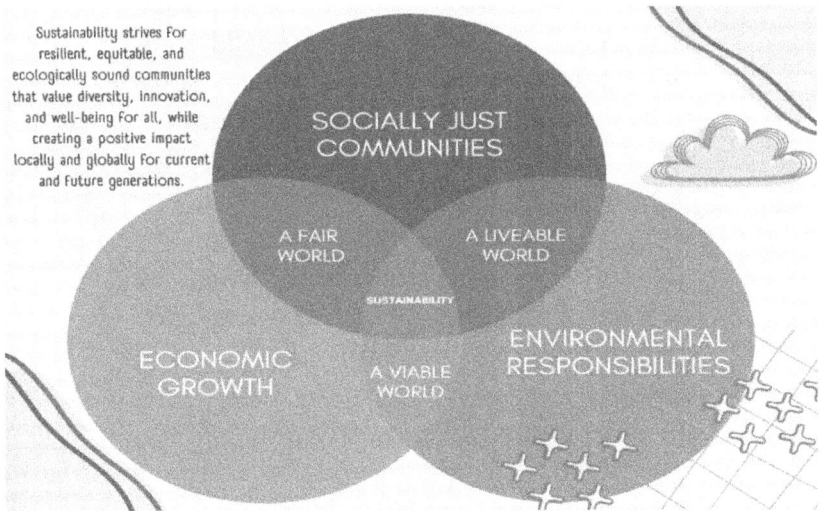

Sustainability strives for resilient, equitable, and ecologically sound communities that value diversity, innovation, and well-being for all, while creating a positive impact locally and globally for current and future generations.

SOCIALLY JUST COMMUNITIES

A FAIR WORLD

A LIVEABLE WORLD

SUSTAINABILITY

ECONOMIC GROWTH

A VIABLE WORLD

ENVIRONMENTAL RESPONSIBILITIES

Although the work of The Homeless Children's Education Fund was crucial, it was met with formidable challenges. Private contributions, grants, and even some backing from the government couldn't save the group from dissolving. This occurred because of reduced financing and shifting priorities.

Despite their best efforts to secure additional funding and continue their work,

The Homeless Children's Education Fund was unable to secure the resources necessary to sustain its services. With the program no longer in operation, a significant gap was left in the support and resources available to homeless children in the Pittsburgh area. This was a devastating blow for the children and families who relied on the program for support and the broader community as a whole.

This story highlights the critical importance of funding for nonprofit organizations and community-based programs. These organizations play a crucial role in addressing critical needs, strengthening communities, promoting equality, fostering innovation, and supporting local economies. Without adequate funding, they could not achieve their mission and serve the communities they care about.

Investing in community-based programming is critical because it empowers communities and provides essential support to those who are most in need. Community empowerment refers to the process of giving people the tools, resources, and opportunities they need to take control of

their own lives and shape their own future.
This is important for several reasons,
including promoting equality and social
justice, strengthening communities,
encouraging active participation, fostering
innovation, and supporting local
economies.

Funding is also essential for supporting
organizations empowering communities
and addressing critical social, economic,
and environmental needs. Adequate
funding provides these organizations the
resources they need to deliver their
programs and services, expand their
programs, build long-term financial stability,
attract and retain high-quality staff and
volunteers, and support their advocacy and
policy change work.

The Homeless Children's Education Fund
was a powerful reminder of the importance
of funding for community-based programs
and their critical role in addressing our
communities' needs. The program's closure
left a significant gap in the support and
resources available to homeless children in
the Pittsburgh area, highlighting the need
for continued investment in these types of

organizations. Without adequate funding, these organizations would not be able to achieve their mission and serve the communities they care about, and the impact would be felt by individuals and communities alike.

Challenge:
Make a difference in your community by taking this challenge: find a local nonprofit or program that aligns with your values and passions, reach out to them to learn how you can support their efforts, make a donation (no matter how small) to help create positive change, and spread the word to encourage others to get involved. With a collective effort, we can empower our communities and build a better future for everyone.

CHAPTER 4

Reimagining Public Safety:
Why Diverting Police Funding is
Critical for Stronger Communities

"The thought of investing in more officers to apprehend murderers only perpetuates a never-ending cycle of violence. It's time we prioritize the well-being of our communities and work towards preventing these tragic killings from occurring in the first place." – Self

Growing up in a neighborhood like many others, I was surrounded by young individuals who possessed immense potential. My friends were driven, charismatic, had excellent organizational and communication skills, and were both creative and persuasive. They had the potential to attend prestigious universities, become successful entrepreneurs, or make a significant impact in their communities.

However, many of my friends ended up channeling their talents toward the streets. This was due to a lack of quality youth programs that offered financial literacy education, mental health support, opportunities, and resources to address problems at home. They sought fast money and respect in a world they knew was rigged against them. Substance abuse and familial difficulties only exacerbated these issues. Over time, their actions caught up with them, leading some to prison, others to an untimely death, and many to a life of poverty and hopelessness.

I saw this same pattern play out in my early professional career as a foster care social worker. Many of my clients had children in foster care, and many of them had been in foster care themselves or came from broken homes. The programs in place were not tailored to each child's individual needs, and often did little more than put a band-aid over deep-seated issues. The lack of quality programming in our communities was all too common, while the NYPD budget was larger than the military budget of some countries.

The consequences of this neglect are devastating. According to the Brennan Center for Justice, youth of color are significantly overrepresented in the juvenile justice system, with Black youth being five times more likely to be incarcerated than white youth. In addition, once incarcerated, these young people face a greater risk of recidivism, perpetuating the cycle of criminalization and neglect.

This issue is not just about numbers and statistics; it goes beyond that. It's about the lives affected, the loss of hope, the injustice perpetuating, and the potential being disregarded. The criminalization and neglect of our communities tear families apart and leave young people without the support they need to reach their full potential.

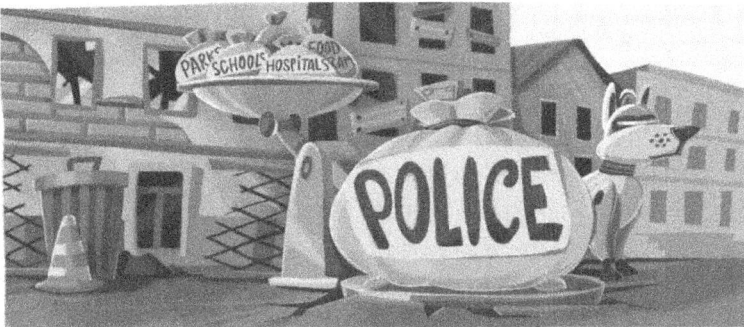

The police budget has been a source of immense controversy and pain in recent years, as communities across the nation struggle with the fact that their hard-earned tax dollars are being invested in a flawed system that perpetuates suffering and injustice. The impact of this over-reliance on policing is felt most acutely in our communities, where individuals are criminalized and neglected, perpetuating a vicious cycle of poverty and hopelessness.

Imagine a world where your neighborhood is heavily patrolled by law enforcement, but the schools are underfunded, and the hospitals are struggling to stay open. This is the reality for many our communities, where the over-reliance on policing has resulted in a cruel cycle of criminalization and neglect.

As the police budget continues to balloon, outpacing other essential services like education and healthcare, our communities are left with nothing but empty promises and shattered dreams. The schools are inadequate, the hospitals are overflowing, and the homes are in disrepair, while the police are given more and more resources to use against the very people they are meant to protect.

In 2022, the NYPD's expense budget reached a historic high of $11.2 billion, surpassing any other police budget in the country. Yet, it's troubling to note that the budget falls short in investing in community-led safety initiatives, despite the strong evidence of their effectiveness in reducing crime rates and building stronger, safer communities.

The results are devastating. In these communities, young people are more likely to be incarcerated than educated, more likely to be homeless than housed, and more likely to be sick than healthy. The inflated police budget has created a "school-to-prison pipeline" that funnels vulnerable youth into the criminal justice system, instead of providing them with the support they need to succeed.

Meanwhile, the police themselves are increasingly prone to abuse and misconduct, further eroding the trust and confidence of the communities they serve. The consequences of this breakdown in trust are far-reaching, as it perpetuates the cycle of criminalization and neglect, leaving our communities to suffer the consequences of a system that was never designed to work for them.

The inflated police budget is not just a matter of numbers and statistics. It's a matter of life and death, of hope and despair, of justice and injustice. It's time for a change, for a new approach that prioritizes the well-being and success of our communities. It's time to divest from a broken system and invest in education, healthcare, housing, and other critical social services that will lift up these communities and break the cycle of criminalization and neglect. The future of our communities depends on it.

The need for alternative approaches to public safety is not just a political or policy debate – it is a moral imperative. The impact of the inflated police budget and the over-reliance on policing is a matter of life and death for our communities. These communities' criminalization and neglect tear families apart and leave individuals with little hope for a brighter future.

Imagine a world where communities are not only safe, but they are also supported and empowered. Imagine a world where children are not funneled into the criminal justice system, but instead receive the education and resources they need to reach their full potential. Imagine a world where individuals experiencing addiction or mental health issues receive the help they need, rather than being incarcerated. This is the world that alternative approaches to public safety can create.

It's time for a change. It's time to reject the notion that more policing and more incarceration are the only solutions to crime. It's time to invest in the well-being and success of our communities, and to support alternative approaches that are based on cooperation, compassion, and a commitment to justice.

The status quo is unacceptable. The inflated police budget and over-reliance on policing have failed our communities for far too long. It's time for a new approach – one that prioritizes the needs and well-being of all people, and that recognizes the value and dignity of every human life. The need for alternative approaches to public safety is clear, and the time to act is now.

The idea of diverting police funding into our communities is one that speaks to the very essence of what it means to be a fair and just society. For far too long, our communities have been disproportionately affected by poverty, violence, and a lack of access to basic resources and opportunities. Meanwhile, the criminal justice system has often failed to address these underlying issues, instead relying on a heavy-handed approach that has led to mass incarceration and a culture of distrust between law enforcement and the communities they serve.

But imagine a world where things were different. Imagine a world where, instead of sending in police officers with weapons and tactics that often escalate tensions, we invested in the well-being and development of our communities. Imagine a world where our communities had access to quality education, healthcare, and job training programs, allowing them to break the cycle of poverty and build better lives for themselves and their families.

In this world, crime rates would likely drop, as people would have the resources they need to thrive and succeed. Tensions between law enforcement and the communities they serve would ease, as trust and cooperation replaced fear and suspicion. And most importantly, our communities would be empowered and uplifted, finally given the resources and opportunities they need to achieve their full potential and lead fulfilling lives.

The benefits of diverting police funding into our communities are not just about reducing crime and improving public safety. They are about creating a more equitable and just society, where all people have the chance to succeed and thrive, regardless of their background or circumstances. This is a powerful and inspiring vision, one that should motivate us all to work towards making it a reality.

Challenge:
Take action today by making your voice heard. Advocate for the reallocation of police funding to community-based programs and nonprofit organizations that focus on providing education, job training, and mental health services to our communities. Reach out to your elected representatives, sign petitions, and participate in community events that promote this important cause. Together, we can help to create a brighter future for our communities and end the cycle of criminalization.

CHAPTER 5

Empowering The Community:
A Journey to Hope & Opportunity through Community Involvement, Partnerships, & Sufficient Funding

"The greatness of a community is most accurately measured by the compassionate actions of its members." – Coretta Scott King

As a social worker, I have seen the devastating impact of programs where governance, leadership, or direct providers do not reflect the individuals and families they serve. I have witnessed young foster children being overmedicated for symptoms like ADHD, and the high turnover of social workers, which takes away precious time from achieving their goals and can be detrimental to clients. As a black man in the field of social services, I also observed the lack of representation of black men, which could have made a huge impact. I knew that I wanted to make a difference and develop tailored programming to create a bigger impact. That is why I set my sights on becoming an executive director of a community-based program.

When I became the executive director of the Martin Luther King Center, one of the oldest and longest running black-led organizations in Long Island, I immediately fell in love with the role. The Long Beach MLK Center offered personal, cultural, athletic, economic, and educational enrichment training to children and adults of all ages, through a system designed to guide, direct, and empower the community.

The center had been on the frontlines, providing support, uplift, and relief to a community that had struggled through adversity and overcome obstacles that challenged the city's most vulnerable residents. I was honored to stand on the shoulders of black activists who had developed the program and to make a huge impact on the North Park area of Long Beach.

However, when I took on the role, the center was closed due to "non-compliance" with the city of Long Beach. Despite this, community organizers, led by the board chair and former staff, continued to fight to get the doors open to serve the community. They understood the significance of the center as a beacon of hope for the community. Meanwhile, the organization was beginning to run out of funding, and as a new executive director, I had to have a difficult conversation with staff about the possibility of a delay in paychecks. To my surprise, the staff was understanding and wanted to support the organization that had an impact not only on the community but on their personal lives as well.

With the support of the board, staff, and community organizers, we were able to overcome this challenge and get the doors open. This was a powerful reminder of the strength and resilience of the community, and of the importance of having sufficient and sustainable funding to support our communities.

The power of community involvement and engagement in supporting our communities cannot be overstated. Community members bring a unique and invaluable perspective and understanding of the challenges and needs of their local area. And their active participation in finding solutions can lead to more effective and lasting outcomes.

EMPOWERING COMMUNITIES FROM WITHIN

THE POWER OF INTERNAL AND EXTERNAL SUPPORT

HIGH EXTERNAL SUPPORT HIGH INTERNAL SUPPORT

This community has received significant external support, including funding, resources, and partnerships. They have also cultivated strong leadership, engaged citizens, and self-sustaining programs. Together, these factors have helped this community to achieve their goals and create lasting change.

HIGH INTERNAL SUPPORT LOW EXTERNAL SUPPORT

This community is strong and resilient, with engaged citizens and self-sustaining programs. However, they lack significant external support, such as funding, resources, or partnerships. With the right support, this community can take their efforts to the next level and create lasting change."

LOW EXTERNAL SUPPORT HIGH INTERNAL SUPPORT

This community has strong leadership, engaged citizens, and self-sustaining programs. They are resilient and self-sufficient, but lack the resources, funding, or partnerships needed to take their efforts to the next level. With external support, this community can amplify their impact and achieve their goals."

LOW INTERNAL SUPPORT LOW EXTERNAL SUPPORT

This community is struggling with limited resources, little engagement, and few opportunities for growth. They lack both internal and external support, which makes it challenging to create meaningful change. However, with the right resources and support, this community has the potential to grow and thrive.

The emotional impact of community involvement and engagement must be acknowledged. When individuals feel that they belong to a community and that their voice is heard, it ignites a sense of purpose and belonging within them. This sense of purpose and belonging can have a profound impact on an individual's self-esteem and overall well-being, especially for our communities who may feel disconnected or disenfranchised from mainstream society. Community involvement and engagement can offer a glimmer of hope and empower these communities to take control of their own future.

Community involvement and engagement fosters a sense of collective responsibility and shared ownership of local issues. When community members are actively involved in addressing challenges and creating solutions, they are more likely to take pride in their community and feel invested in its future. This sense of shared responsibility can strengthen community bonds and foster a stronger sense of community identity.

Data supports the vital role that community involvement and engagement play in creating positive change for our communities. A study by the Harvard Kennedy School found that community-based programs that involve local residents in decision-making and implementation lead to more successful and sustainable outcomes. The study found that community-based programs were more effective in addressing local challenges and had a greater impact on community well-being when compared to programs solely implemented by external organizations.

Another study by the National Civic League found that communities with high levels of civic engagement and community involvement were more likely to tackle social and economic challenges, resulting in improved quality of life for residents. The study found that communities with high levels of community involvement had lower poverty rates, better educational outcomes, and improved health outcomes.

The availability of sufficient and sustainable funding can be the difference between struggling to survive and thriving. Providing these communities with the resources and support they need to improve their quality of life is a crucial step in empowering them and giving them hope for a better future.

Insight into the emotional significance of reliable finance is critical. People in our communities get a sense of worth and agency when they have access to the tools and support they need to thrive. They have faith that their needs will be provided for and that their well-being will be prioritized. A person's self-esteem and happiness may greatly benefit from this degree of control and acceptance. It can provide a glimmer of hope and a brighter future for those who have faced systemic barriers and challenges.

In addition, tackling the causes of poverty and inequality in our communities may benefit greatly from substantial and secure investment. We can help our communities break the cycle of poverty and create a better future for themselves and future generations by improving their access to education, healthcare, and economic opportunities. To realize one's full potential and improve one's quality of life, these tools may well be invaluable.

Data supports the importance of providing sufficient and sustainable funding to our communities. A study by the Urban Institute found that communities with higher levels of public investment in education, health care, and economic development had lower poverty rates and improved health outcomes. The study found that public investment in these areas led to increased access to resources and support for our communities, resulting in improved quality of life.

Additionally, a study by the National Bureau of Economic Research found that government programs that provide financial assistance to low-income individuals and families can have a positive impact on their well-being and financial stability. The study found that these programs can improve access to education, health care, and economic opportunities, leading to a brighter future for our communities.

We can help our communities become self-reliant and hopeful by giving them access to stable funding. Our communities will feel more respected and empowered, they will be able to escape the cycle of poverty, and they will be able to create a better future for themselves and future generations if they have access to the resources and assistance they need. The significance of adequate and dependable financing in bringing about meaningful change in our communities is backed up by data. By putting money into these areas, we can make the world a better, more just place for everyone.

Challenge:
Take action in your own community. Reach out to local organizations and see how you can get involved in supporting communities. Whether it's volunteering your time, donating resources, or advocating for change, your actions can make a positive impact and empower these communities to shape their own future. Join the journey towards empowerment and hope for our communities and see the difference you can make.

CHAPTER 6

<u>Rising Above The Resistance:</u>
A Path Toward Justice & Equality
For Our Communities

"We cannot solve our problems with the same thinking we used when we created them." – Albert Einstein

The year 2020 was a turning point in the fight for justice and equality. The brutal killings of Breonna Taylor, Ahmad Abrey, and George Floyd at the hands of the police sparked a wave of protests and demonstrations that echoed across the nation and the world. The cries of "Black Lives Matter" resonated with people from all walks of life who were fed up with the systemic racism and police brutality that had plagued communities of color for far too long.

However, this movement also sparked a countermovement, as the phrase "Blue Lives Matter" emerged in response, symbolizing support for the police and opposition to the protests. This countermovement was made up of some members of law enforcement and their supporters, as well as resistance from government and law enforcement agencies themselves. Police unions, for example, have been known to resist reforms aimed at increasing accountability and reducing police violence. This resistance takes the form of opposition to legislation, lawsuits, or public statements, and serves as a reminder of the deep divisions and obstacles that stand in the way of progress.

As a melting pot of diverse communities and perspectives, this division was particularly evident in New York City. In neighborhoods like Bay Ridge and Staten Island, one could see the iconic black and grey American flag with the blue line down the middle, along with Trump 2020 logos, displayed proudly on cars, homes, and clothing. This sight was a stark reminder of the ongoing struggle and division, and left many feeling uneasy and fearful for their safety.

Despite these efforts to resist change, communities of color continue to push for transparency and accountability within the criminal justice system. The initial response of painting "BLACK LIVES MATTER" on the streets, while symbolic, was seen by many as a superficial gesture, rather than a commitment to real and lasting change. The skepticism and distrust of the government, combined with previous negative experiences with law enforcement, only heightens the urgency for meaningful and impactful reforms.

The struggle for change and justice in our communities often faces significant resistance from the police and government. This resistance can take many forms, ranging from overt opposition to more subtle forms of obstruction. Regardless of the form it takes, police and government resistance can have a profound and devastating impact on our communities and their efforts to create positive change.

Mack Graham

The emotional toll of police and government resistance cannot be overstated. For our communities, the fight for justice and equality can feel like an uphill battle, especially when faced with opposition from those who are meant to protect and serve them. The experience of being targeted, profiled, and dehumanized by the police and government can lead to feelings of hopelessness, anger, and frustration, which can further exacerbate already existing social and economic challenges.

Data supports the reality of police and government resistance in our communities. A study by the American Civil Liberties Union (ACLU) found that black Americans are disproportionately targeted and subjected to police violence, regardless of their level of involvement in criminal activity. The study found that black Americans are 2.5 times more likely to be killed by the police than their white counterparts, and are also more likely to be subjected to excessive use of force, even in non-threatening situations.

Moreover, a study by the National Institute of Justice found that police and government resistance to change can take many forms, including the failure to implement policies and practices that address racial profiling and the use of excessive force. The study found that this resistance can also include the failure to hold police officers accountable for their actions and the lack of transparency and accountability in police departments.

Addressing resistance from the police and government is a crucial step in creating positive change for our communities. By speaking out against police violence and demanding accountability and transparency, our communities can make their voices heard and push for meaningful change. Additionally, by building partnerships with community organizations and advocacy groups, our communities can amplify their message and increase their impact.

The emotional significance of overcoming police and government resistance cannot be overstated. When our communities are able to overcome this resistance, they feel empowered and validated. They know that their voices are being heard and that their struggle for justice and equality is being taken seriously. This sense of empowerment and validation can have a profound and lasting impact on our communities, giving them hope for a better future and inspiring them to continue their fight for change.

Data supports the importance of overcoming police and government resistance in creating positive change for our communities. A study by the Department of Justice found that communities with strong partnerships between law enforcement and community organizations had lower rates of crime and improved relationships between the police and the community. The study found that when police officers are held accountable, transparent, and communities are involved in the decision-making process, it leads to a safer and more just community for all.

To bring about constructive change in our communities, we must first overcome opposition from police and government. It is possible for communities to make their voices heard and effect real change if they speak out against police brutality and demand accountability and transparency from local police forces. To say that overcoming this opposition is emotionally significant is an understatement, and evidence backs up the value of our effort in making the world a safer, more just, and more egalitarian place for everyone.

When working towards creating positive change for our communities, it's important to understand that there will be obstacles that must be overcome. These obstacles can come from various sources, including resistance from the police and government, as well as from within our communities themselves. But keep in mind that every challenge can be met head-on with enough resourcefulness, determination, and openness to new ideas.

The police and government can often represent significant obstacles to change, as they have the power to enforce laws and policies that may be harmful to our communities. This resistance can take many forms, from actively blocking progress to passively ignoring the needs of our communities. It can be disheartening and discouraging to face such resistance, but it's important to remember that change is possible, even in the face of these obstacles.

One way to overcome resistance from the police and government is by finding creative solutions that work within the existing system. This may involve building relationships and partnerships with government officials and law enforcement, leveraging media and public opinion to bring attention to the issues facing our communities, or using data and research to demonstrate the need for change. By approaching these obstacles with creativity and a willingness to find new solutions, it's possible to make progress and create positive change for our communities.

In addition to facing resistance from the police and government, it's also important to address resistance from within our communities themselves. This can take many forms, from a lack of trust in government and law enforcement, to a lack of interest in participating in community activism and advocacy. To overcome these internal obstacles, it's important to build strong relationships with community members, to understand their perspectives and concerns, and to provide them with the resources and support they need to get involved and make a difference.

By exploring creative solutions and addressing resistance from both the police and government and within our communities, lasting and meaningful change can be achieved for our communities. Community-based policing is one such solution that offers hope for a brighter future.

This approach is rooted in the belief that trust and collaboration between law enforcement and the communities they serve is crucial for promoting positive change. By involving community members in the policing process and giving their input and feedback a priority, a sense of shared responsibility and mutual respect is fostered. This can take the form of community meetings, youth programs, and partnerships with local organizations and has the potential to reduce tensions and promote lasting change.

The use of technology is another powerful tool in the fight for justice and equality. Body cameras that do not cut off, early warning systems, and online portals for accessing police records and complaint data are just a few of the innovative solutions that are increasing public trust in law enforcement and providing a clearer picture of what is happening on the ground. These solutions offer a glimmer of hope in the ongoing fight for a more just and equitable society.

It is important to remember that change is possible, and that the power to create positive change lies within us all. Whether through advocacy, education, community building, or any other approach, let us work towards creating a brighter future for our communities.

Challenge:
Take some time today to actively listen to someone you interact with. This could be a friend, family member, co-worker, or even a stranger. Really focus on what they are saying and try to understand their

perspective without interrupting or trying to steer the conversation in a different direction. When they finish speaking, take a moment to reflect on what you heard and try to summarize their thoughts back to them. This simple act of active listening can help to build empathy, understanding, and strengthen relationships. So go ahead and give it a try!

CHAPTER 7

Building a Better World:
A Call to Action for Justice and Equity

"It is our duty to fight for our freedom. It is our duty to win. We must love each other and support each other. We have nothing to lose but our chains." - Assata Shakur

In 2016, I returned to New York to finish grad school. I had the urge to join a social justice organization after feeling the weight of the injustices against Black lives that were plaguing America in the wake of the killings of Mike Brown, Trayvon Martin, and Eric Garner. The murder of these men sent a shockwave throughout the nation, and their deaths ignited the flame in me to fight for justice.

While in Texas, I deeply desired to be on the street and involved in my hometown's social justice campaigns. It was a feeling that was hard to ignore, as it seemed like every day, there was another story of a Black person who was killed or mistreated by the police. It was a feeling of helplessness that I couldn't shake. I knew that I had to do something.

Upon returning to New York, I began reaching out to various social justice organizations to get involved. One in particular stood out to me, The Gathering for Justice. Founded by Harry Belafonte, the organization's mission is to build a movement to end child incarceration while working to eliminate the racial inequities that permeate policing and the justice system. Their approach was intersectional, and they infused art, culture, and creative practices to build and sustain a nonviolent justice movement. The Gathering for Justice also developed leadership rooted in historical wisdom, which inspired me to join them.

It was through The Gathering for Justice that I learned that understanding my role in the movement for justice is crucial for several reasons. Knowing my role helped to clarify my objectives and priorities within the movement, allowing me to focus my energy and resources effectively. Understanding my role also helped me to work effectively with others in the movement, as I had a clear understanding of how my actions fit into the larger picture. By knowing my role, I could take responsibility for my actions and be held accountable for the impact that they had on the movement.

Moreover, knowing my role helped me to effectively advocate for the causes that I cared about, as I had a clear understanding of the issues and the most effective ways to address them. Understanding my role also empowered me as an activist, as I had a clear understanding of the ways in which I could make a difference and contribute to the movement for justice.

The journey was far from easy, as I faced numerous challenges, both personally and in my work with The Gathering for Justice. Initially, I was unsure of how to utilize my skills to make the greatest impact, and I struggled with finding my place in this important movement. But with time and persistence, I was able to find my footing. I was fortunate enough to have a supportive community of passionate, innovative, smart individuals. It was a process of trial and error, but I learned to trust my instincts and the value of my contributions. Through my experiences, I realized the importance of a strong support system and how crucial it is to have allies who uplift and amplify our voices.

One of the most challenging experiences was during the 2020 uprising. The protests were in response to the brutal murder of George Floyd, a Black man who was killed by a white police officer. The protests quickly escalated, and we had to find a way to channel our anger and frustration into something productive. It was during this time that we really had to lock in on being able to support from all avenues.

People were actively protesting on the street. If people had the means to give financially, they were donating money to organizations. If they were afraid to go outside because of the pandemic or afraid to get involved in protests, they shared information online or made calls to various elected officials to advocate for policy change. This concerted effort led to us coming together to make a huge impact.

On June 6, 2020, we raised our voices and hit the streets of New York City for The March for Stolen Loves and Looted Dreams. We made serval demands. One of the key demands was for the repeal of 50-A, the Police Secrecy Law. This law, which had been in place in New York since 1976, allowed police officers to shield their disciplinary records from the public. This lack of transparency made it difficult for communities to hold officers accountable for misconduct or use-of-force incidents.

As a result of the advocacy efforts of The Gathering for Justice and other organizations, New York Governor Andrew Cuomo signed the repeal of 50-A into law on June 12, 2020. This bill now requires police departments across the state to disclose officers' disciplinary records, including any complaints filed against them.

Another demand was for the city to cut the NYPD budget and redirect funds to safety nets and key needs for Black and Brown communities. The NYPD budget has been a source of controversy for many years, with critics arguing that it is too large and that the funds could be better spent on other community needs.

During the 2020 fiscal year, the NYPD's budget exceeded the combined spending of the health department, homeless services, and youth and community development, totaling an astonishing $5.2 billion. Despite widespread calls for a major budget reduction, the final budget for the 2021 fiscal year was only cut by around 1%. As outlined in Chapter 4, the NYPD's budget has ballooned, reaching an unprecedented $11.2 billion in 2022.

Another demand was for the passage of the Anti-Chokehold Bill, which would criminalize the use of chokeholds by police officers. Chokeholds have been a controversial tactic used by police officers for many years, with critics arguing that they are inherently dangerous and can lead to serious injury or death.

Mack Graham

The bill was passed by the New York City Council in June 2020. It requires officers to face a misdemeanor charge and a maximum of one year in jail if they use a chokehold during an arrest.

Finally, The Gathering for Justice and Justice League NYC demanded that the NYPD hold officers accountable for their actions, not only when they kill Black people, but when they disproportionately target them for arrests in subways and when they use racist programs like Broken Windows.

Broken Windows is a policing strategy that targets minor offenses, such as vandalism or fare evasion, as a way of preventing more serious crimes. Critics argue that the strategy disproportionately targets Black and Brown communities, resulting in unnecessary arrests and harassment.

The Gathering for Justice and Justice League NYC demanded that the NYPD end the use of Broken Windows and hold officers accountable for any discriminatory practices. By advocating for these policies and demanding change, The Gathering for Justice and Justice League NYC worked to create a more just and equitable society for all.

The work we did was imperative, and we needed support to strive. However, I also realized that support did not need to be financial; active volunteering was incredibly helpful, whether it was assisting with events or promoting via social media. During the 2020 uprising, we really had to lock in on being able to support from all avenues. Those who went to the streets to protest did so vigorously. Those who were in a position to do so were undoubtedly providing financial support to various causes. They spread information online or called different public officials to urge policy change if they were too fearful of going outside due to the pandemic or participating in rallies. This concerted effort led to us coming together to make a huge impact.

The Gathering for Justice and Justice League NYC and CA state task forces have utilized Kingian nonviolence as a powerful social application for systemic change and civic engagement. Through their work, Justice League NYC and Justice League CA have brought together juvenile and criminal justice experts, advocates, artists, and individuals directly impacted by incarceration and state violence to build an agenda for sustained Black and Brown liberation. This work reminds us of the urgency to take action and build a more just and equitable society for all. Systemic oppression has been deeply rooted in our society for centuries, but each one of us has the power to challenge it. Every small action we take, no matter how insignificant it may seem, can significantly impact our communities' lives and help build a better world.

The importance of taking action cannot be overstated. For far too long, our communities have been denied access to resources, opportunities, and basic human rights. The statistics are staggering: Black Americans are 2.5 times more likely to be killed by police than white Americans. They are also more likely to be incarcerated and receive longer sentences for the same crimes. Native Americans experience some of the highest rates of poverty, unemployment, and suicide in the country. The LGBTQ+ community faces discrimination and violence daily. These are just a few examples of the deep-seated inequality that exists in our society.

However, it is not enough to simply acknowledge these injustices. We must take action to address them, and there are many ways to get involved in the fight for justice and equity. One critical step is to educate ourselves on the history and impact of systematic oppression. Reading books, articles, and academic papers, as well as attending workshops and seminars led by experts in the field, can deepen our understanding and help us become more effective advocates for change.

Another powerful way to take action is to support community-led initiatives. Grassroots organizations and services that are run by and for our communities have a deep understanding of the unique challenges faced by those communities and are often best equipped to address them. Donating money or time to these organizations, attending their events, and amplifying their voices on social media can all make a significant difference.

Mack Graham

Getting involved with community-led initiatives and organizations, whether it's following them on social media or volunteering, is a great way to increase awareness of the issues they advocate for. In New York City, criminal justice organizations promote the How Many Stops Act, which aims to improve transparency in the NYPD's daily activities. This act includes two bills that require the NYPD to report on police street stops, investigative encounters, and consent searches. By enhancing police transparency and accountability, safeguarding the Right to Know Act, and reducing discriminatory policing practices that harm communities of color, these bills are essential for building a more just and equitable society.

In addition to getting involved, we can use our voice and vote to elect officials prioritizing justice and equity. Researching candidates and their platforms, and voting in every election, no matter how small, can help create meaningful change. Speaking up against injustices, calling out racism, homophobia, transphobia, and other forms of discrimination, and advocating for policies and practices that promote equality and justice for all are all crucial steps that we can take.

Diverting police funding into our communities is also a critical step toward creating a more just and equitable society. We know that the current system of policing is failing our communities, and we need alternative approaches to public safety. By investing in community-based solutions, we can reduce harm and promote healing. We can create a world where everyone is safe and valued, regardless of their race, gender, or social status.

However, we also know that there will be resistance. There will be resistance from the police and government, and there may even be resistance from within our communities. Overcoming these obstacles will not be easy, but we cannot allow them to discourage us. We must find creative solutions to overcome these obstacles and continue to work tirelessly towards creating a more just and equitable society.

Creating a more just and equitable society is not just a moral imperative; it is also an economic one. Research has shown that inequality is bad for everyone, not just those who are directly affected by it. Countries with higher levels of inequality tend to have lower levels of economic growth, as well as higher levels of social unrest, crime, and health problems. By investing in our communities and creating a more just and equitable society, we can not only improve the lives of those who have been historically disenfranchised, but we can also create a better future for all of us.

In conclusion, the fight for justice and equity is a long and difficult one, but it is also one of the most important fights of our time. It is a fight for the soul of our society, and for the dignity and well-being of every person within it. We must be prepared for the long haul, and we must be willing to do the hard work that is necessary to bring about meaningful change.

However, we should keep in mind that the struggle for equal opportunity and social justice is not something that can be accomplished by a single person or group. It will require a collective effort from all of us, from every corner of society. We must work together to build bridges between communities, listen to each other's perspectives, and find common ground. We must be willing to learn from each other, to grow and evolve as individuals and as a society, and to hold ourselves accountable when we fall short.

The journey toward justice and equity will be marked by both successes and setbacks, but we must not be discouraged by the obstacles that we face. We must remember that progress is possible and that every small step forward is a step toward a better world. We must have faith in our ability to create change and build a more just and equitable society for all.

In the end, in the battle for justice and fairness, it is not enough to just treat the symptoms of systemic oppression; we must also get to the root of its causes. It is about challenging the fundamental structures and beliefs that have allowed inequality to thrive and about creating a world that is truly just and equitable for all. It is a fight for a world where every person has the opportunity to live a fulfilling and dignified life, free from discrimination, fear, and oppression.

So, let us, as Neighborhood Hope Dealerz, take up the challenge, let us take action, and let us work together to build a more just and equitable society for all. Let us be the generation of Neighborhood Hope Dealerz that rises to the occasion, that refuses to accept the status quo, and that creates a better world for ourselves and for future generations. Together, as Neighborhood Hope Dealerz, we can make a difference, and together, as Neighborhood Hope Dealerz, we can build a world that is truly just and equitable for all.

Challenge:
I challenge you to take action toward building a more just and equitable society. As a neighborhood hope dealer, you can make a significant impact by educating yourself on the impact of systemic oppression, supporting community-led initiatives, using your voice and vote to advocate for change, and diverting police funding into our communities. Remember that the fight for justice and equity is a collective effort, and every small step forward is a step towards a better world.

Let us work together as neighborhood hope dealerz to challenge the fundamental structures and beliefs that allow inequality to thrive and create a world that is truly just and equitable for all.

APPENDIX

The Hope Dealerz Toolkit:
Resources for Learning, Action, and Self-Care

Mack Graham

Empowering Communities from Within: A Comprehensive Guide to Building a Nonprofit

You know the struggles your community faces daily. You see the injustices and the disparities. You know there is a need for change and you have the power to create it. Starting a nonprofit can be a powerful way to empower your community and make a positive impact.

This guide will walk you through the steps to start a nonprofit that focuses on transforming your community from within. We'll help you find the passion, dedication, and strength to make a change.

Step 1: Define Your Mission and Vision
You are the best advocate for your community, so start by defining your mission and vision. Your mission and vision should be specific, inspiring, and actionable. Identify the problems and challenges your community faces and envision a better future.

a) Identify your community's problems and challenges: Spend time researching and reflecting on the issues impacting your community. This could involve talking to community members, reviewing data and statistics, and observing what's happening around you.

b) Envision a better future: Once you've identified the challenges, think about what a better future could look like. What kind of changes would you like to see? What impact would you like to make?

c) Be specific: Your mission and vision should be clear and specific. Rather than using vague or general language, focus on describing your goals in concrete and measurable terms. This will help you stay focused and hold yourself accountable.

d) Be inspiring: Your mission and vision should be compelling and inspiring. It should speak to the values and aspirations of your community and inspire others to get involved.

e) Be actionable: Your mission and vision should be actionable. This means that it should describe specific steps or actions that you will take to achieve your goals. This will help you stay focused and make progress toward your vision.

f) Refine and revise: Defining your mission and vision is an iterative process. You may need to refine and revise your goals as you learn more about your community and what's possible. Be open to feedback and be willing to make changes as needed.

Step 2: Create a Business Plan

Once you have a clear mission and vision, create a business plan to guide your nonprofit. A good business plan should include goals, strategies, and resources needed to achieve them. You should also define your target audience, the needs you aim to address, and how you'll measure your success.

a) Set your goals: Define your goalsand how you plan to achieve them. Be specific about what you want to accomplish and how you will measure success. This will help you stay focused and stay on track.

b) Define your target audience and needs: Identify your target audience and the needs you aim to address. This will help you create programs and services that are aligned with your mission, and that will make a meaningful impact in your community.

c) Determine your resources: Determine the resources needed to achieve your goals, such as funding, volunteers, and partnerships. This will help you identify gaps and plan accordingly.

d) Develop strategies: Develop strategies to achieve your goals, such as fundraising, community outreach, and program development. Be creative and think outside the box to find new ways to impact your community.

e) Measure success: Develop metrics to measure your success, such as the number of people served, the amount of money raised, and the impact of your programs. This will help you stay accountable and adjust your strategies as needed.

Step 3: Incorporate Your Nonprofit
Incorporating your nonprofit is a legal requirement to start your organization. You'll need to register with your state's nonprofit authority and apply for tax-exempt status with the IRS. This process involves filing articles of incorporation, obtaining a tax ID, and creating bylaws.

   a) Choose a name for your nonprofit: Pick a name that is clear, concise, and relevant to your mission.
   b) Check availability: Check with your state's nonprofit authority to ensure your chosen name is available and doesn't conflict with any existing trademarks or names.
   c) Create your articles of incorporation: Your articles of incorporation should outline your nonprofit's purpose, governance structure, and other important details. This legal document must be filed with your state's nonprofit authority.
   d) Obtain a tax identification number: You'll need a tax identification

number (TIN) to open a bank account, apply for tax-exempt status, and perform other administrative tasks. You can apply for a TIN with the IRS online.

e) Create bylaws: Your bylaws outline how your nonprofit will be governed, including how board members will be elected and what their responsibilities are.

f) File your paperwork: Once you've completed your articles of incorporation and bylaws, file them with your state's nonprofit authority. This will officially incorporate your nonprofit.

g) Apply for tax-exempt status: To become a tax-exempt organization, you'll need to file Form 1023 or Form 1023-EZ with the IRS. This process can take several months, so plan accordingly.

h) Register for state and local taxes: Depending on where you operate, you may need to register for state and local taxes like sales or property taxes.

i) Open a bank account: To keep your nonprofit's finances separate from your personal finances, open a bank account in your nonprofit's name.

Step 4: Recruit a Board of Directors
Your board of directors is responsible for guiding and overseeing your nonprofit. A strong board should include people with financial, legal, and marketing expertise, as well as members with strong community connections. Look for people who share your passion and bring diverse skills and perspectives.

    a) Define the role and responsibilities of your board: Before you start recruiting board members, it's important to have a clear understanding of their roles and responsibilities. This includes establishing board member expectations, such as meeting attendance, committee participation, and fundraising responsibilities.

    b) Develop a list of potential board members: Look for people who are passionate about your mission and who have expertise in areas that will be valuable to your organization. Consider reaching out to people in

your professional network, as well
as members of your community who
are involved in related
organizations.

c) Assess potential board members:
Once you have a list of potential
board members, assess each
candidate's qualifications and fit
with your organization. Consider
their professional expertise,
experience serving on other boards,
and their level of engagement with
your community.

d) Conduct interviews: Meet with each
potential board member to discuss
their interest in your organization,
their qualifications, and their goals
for serving on the board. Be
prepared to answer their questions
about the organization and its
mission.

e) Extend an invitation: Once you have
identified the most qualified
candidates, extend an invitation to
join your board. Make sure that they
understand the time commitment
and expectations associated with
board service, and provide them

with an orientation to the organization.

f) Provide ongoing support: Board members need ongoing support to be effective in their roles. Provide regular training and education opportunities and opportunities for networking and collaboration with other board members and stakeholders.

Step 5: Develop Programs and Services
Your programs should be designed to address your community's needs and align with your mission and vision. Conduct research to develop evidence-based programs that have been proven effective in other communities. Be open to feedback from your community and adapt your programs accordingly.

a) Conduct research: Identify the needs and challenges your community faces, and conduct research to determine evidence-based programs that have been successful in other communities facing similar challenges.

b) Develop your programs: Once you have identified the needs and challenges faced by your community, develop your programs and services to address them. Ensure that your programs are aligned with your mission and vision and are evidence-based.

c) Pilot test your programs: Before launching your programs, pilot test them to identify any potential issues and get feedback from your community. Use this feedback to make improvements and refine your programs.

d) Create a program evaluation plan: Develop a program evaluation plan to track the progress of your programs and measure their impact. Identify the key metrics you will use to measure success, and establish a timeline for evaluation.

e) Continuously improve your programs: Use the results of your program evaluations to continuously improve your programs. Adapt your programs based on your community's feedback and your evaluations' results.

f) Collaborate with other organizations: Partner with other

organizations to leverage their expertise and resources in developing and delivering your programs. Look for organizations that share your values and are committed to positively impacting your community.

Step 6: Fundraise and Build Partnerships
Fundraising is critical to the success of your nonprofit. Develop a fundraising strategy that includes grant writing, individual giving, and corporate partnerships. Build partnerships with organizations that share your values and mission. Collaborating with other groups can help amplify your impact.

a) Develop a fundraising plan: Create a plan that outlines your fundraising goals and strategies for achieving them. Your plan should include various fundraising methods such as grant writing, individual donations, and corporate partnerships.

b) Identify potential funders: Research foundations, corporations, and government agencies that fund organizations like yours. Make a list of potential funders and identify which ones align with your mission and values.

c) Create a case for support: Develop a compelling case for why people should donate to your nonprofit. Use stories, statistics, and other evidence to show the impact your organization is making in the community.

d) Cultivate relationships with donors: Develop relationships with individual donors and major donors. Keep them updated on your organization's progress and the impact of their donations.

e) Apply for grants: Apply for grants from foundations, corporations, and government agencies. Research each funder's requirements and tailor your application to their priorities and goals.

f) Host fundraising events: Plan and host fundraising events to raise money and awareness for your nonprofit. These events could be virtual or in-person, and could include auctions, charity walks, or benefit concerts.

g) Build partnerships: Identify organizations that share your mission and values, and explore opportunities for collaboration. Building partnerships can help amplify your impact and make your organization more effective in achieving its goals.

h) Cultivate relationships with partners: Develop relationships with partners and keep them updated on your organization's progress. Collaborate on projects and initiatives to increase the impact of your work.

i) Show appreciation: Show appreciation to your donors and partners by thanking them for their support. This could include sending thank-you notes, hosting appreciation events, or recognizing them on your website or social media.

Step 7: Evaluate and Improve

As you implement your programs, collect data on your outcomes and analyze them to improve them. Share your impact with your stakeholders and the community to build trust and engagement.

a) Identify the outcomes you want to achieve: Before implementing your programs, identify the specific outcomes you want to achieve. What do you hope to accomplish? What metrics will you use to measure success?

b) Track your progress: Once you have identified your outcomes, track your progress using data. Collect data on key performance indicators, such as the number of people served or the percentage of participants who achieve specific goals.

c) Analyze your data: Use your data to evaluate your programs and identify areas for improvement. Are you achieving your outcomes? What is working well and what needs to change?

d) Make changes: Based on your analysis, make changes to your programs to improve their effectiveness. Consider new approaches or modifications to existing ones to better meet the needs of your community.

e) Communicate your impact: Share your successes and challenges with your stakeholders, including your board, funders, and the community. Communicate the impact of your programs and the changes you are making to continuously improve. This can help build trust and engagement with those who support your work.

Remember, evaluating and improving your nonprofit's impact is an ongoing process. By continuously tracking your progress and making changes as necessary, you can build a strong and effective organization that truly empowers your community from within.

Empowering Communities: 40 Rolling Grant Opportunities

AllPeople: Grants for community development, social justice, and environmental causes. Grant amount: Varies. Giving areas: Education, environment, health, human services, and civic engagement. Apply at: allpeople.co.

Awesome Foundation: Micro-grants for innovative and creative community projects. Grant amount: $1,000. Giving areas: Arts, education, environment, health, and social issues. Apply at: awesomefoundation.org.

Ben & Jerry's Foundation: Grants for grassroots community organizing and social justice advocacy. Grant amount: Varies. Giving areas: Environmental justice, social justice, and supporting family farms. Apply at: benandjerrysfoundation.org.

The Pollination Project: Grants for grassroots community initiatives and individual projects. Grant amount: $1,000. Giving areas: Animal welfare, community building, environmental sustainability, health and wellness, human rights, and social justice. Apply at: thepollinationproject.org.

The Seed Fund: Grants for creative and innovative ideas for social change. Grant amount: $500. Giving areas: Community development, education, environment, health, and social justice. Apply at: seedfundgrants.com.

The Awesome Without Borders: Grants for initiatives that inspire awe and spark wonder. Grant amount: $1,000. Giving areas: Education, environment, health, human services, and the arts. Apply at: awesomewithoutborders.org.

Patagonia Grant Program: Grants for grassroots environmental organizations. Grant amount: Varies. Giving areas: Environmental protection and conservation. Apply at: patagonia.com/grant-guidelines.html.

The Pollard Foundation: Grants for organizations focused on education, poverty reduction, and social justice. Grant amount: Varies. Giving areas: Education, poverty reduction, and social justice. Apply at: pollardfoundation.org/grant-guidelines.

The Rose Foundation: Grants for grassroots environmental initiatives. Grant amount: Varies. Giving areas: Environmental protection and conservation. Apply at: rosefdn.org/grants-programs/grants.

The Threshold Foundation: Grants for social and environmental change initiatives. Grant amount: Varies. Giving areas: Economic justice, environmental sustainability, and social justice. Apply at: thresholdfoundation.org/grants.

Urgent Action Fund: Rapid response grants for women's rights and social justice initiatives. Grant amount: Varies. Giving areas: Women's rights, human rights, and social justice. Apply at: urgentactionfund.org.

The Wege Foundation: Grants for environmental and social justice initiatives. Grant amount: Varies. Giving areas: Environment, education, arts, and health care. Apply at: wegefoundation.com/grants.

The Anne Ray Charitable Trust: Grants for social and environmental justice initiatives. Grant amount: Varies. Giving areas: Environment, education, arts, and health care. Apply at: anneraytrust.org/apply.

Building Equity & Alignment for Impact Fund: Grants for community-led organizations and initiatives focused on equity and justice. Grant amount: Varies. Giving areas: Equity and justice. Apply at: bea4impact.org.

The Chorus Foundation: Grants for environmental justice initiatives. Grant amount: Varies. Giving areas: Environmental justice. Apply at: chorusfoundation.org/grants.

United Way: Provides grants to nonprofits working in areas such as education, financial stability, and health. Apply through your local United Way chapter.

Starbucks Foundation: Provides grants to nonprofits working in areas such as job training, education, and community development. Apply at

starbucks.com/responsibility/community/gr
ant-funding.

Mary Reynolds Babcock Foundation:
Provides grants to nonprofits in the
Southeastern US working in areas such as
community development, education, and
economic justice. Apply at mrf.org/grants.

Foundation for Rural Service: Provides
grants to nonprofits in rural areas working
in areas such as education, economic
development, and healthcare. Apply at
frs.org.

**American Association of University
Women**: Provides grants to nonprofits
working in areas such as gender equity,
education, and economic security. Apply at
aauw.org.

W.K. Kellogg Foundation: Provides grants
to nonprofits working in areas such as
education, health, and racial equity. Apply
at wkkf.org.

Ford Foundation: Provides grants to
nonprofits working in areas such as human

rights, economic justice, and democracy. Apply at fordfoundation.org.

Nathan Cummings Foundation: Provides grants to nonprofits working in areas such as environmental sustainability, social justice, and economic fairness. Apply at nathancummings.org.

Andrew W. Mellon Foundation: Provides grants to nonprofits working in areas such as higher education, cultural institutions, and the arts. Apply at mellon.org.

Knight Foundation: Provides grants to nonprofits working in areas such as journalism, arts and culture, and community engagement. Apply at knightfoundation.org.

Open Society Foundations: Provides grants to nonprofits working in areas such as human rights, democratic governance, and social justice. Apply at opensocietyfoundations.org.

Robert Wood Johnson Foundation: Provides grants to nonprofits working in areas such as healthcare, public health, and social determinants of health. Apply at rwjf.org.

Mozilla Foundation: Provides grants to nonprofits working in areas such as internet access, privacy, and open source software. Apply at foundation.mozilla.org.

Conrad N. Hilton Foundation: Provides grants to nonprofits working in areas such as homelessness, substance abuse, and disaster relief. Apply at hiltonfoundation.org.

PNC Foundation: Provides grants to nonprofits working in areas such as education, the arts, and community development. Apply at pnc.com.

Robert R. McCormick Foundation: Provides grants to nonprofits working in areas such as education, journalism, and veterans affairs. Apply at mccormickfoundation.org.

Walton Family Foundation: Provides grants to nonprofits working in areas such as education, the environment, and economic development. Apply at waltonfamilyfoundation.org.

Kresge Foundation: Provides grants to nonprofits working in areas such as community development, education, and the arts. Apply at kresge.org.

Joyce Foundation: Provides grants to nonprofits working in areas such as education, democracy, and the environment. Apply at joycefdn.org.

Lilly Endowment: Provides grants to nonprofits working in areas such as education, religion, and community development. Apply at lillyendowment.org.

Echoing Green: Provides seed-stage funding and support to emerging leaders working on social change projects. To apply echoinggreen.org/fellowship.

Brown Foundation: Provides grants to support nonprofit organizations working in the areas of education, community development, and the arts. Apply at brownfoundation.org/grants/how-to-apply/.

Global Fund for Women: Provides grants to support women-led organizations working to advance women's rights and gender equality around the world. Apply at globalfundforwomen.org/apply-for-a-grant/.

Surdna Foundation: Support social justice, sustainable environments, and inclusive economies. Apply at surdna.org.

Threshold Foundation: Supports social, economic, and environmental justice through a range of grants and fellowship programs. Apply at thresholdfoundation.org.

Illuminating the Dark Legacy of Systematic Oppression: 22 Powerful Books and Articles

Books:

"State of Emergency: How We Win in the Country We Built" by Tamika Mallory – This book is a powerful and inspiring book that provides strategies and insights on how to address issues such as police brutality, gun violence, and racism in the United States

"We Are Not Here to Be Bystanders: A Memoir of Love and Resistance" by Linda Sarsour – This book is a courageous and moving memoir that highlights the role of identity and intersectionality in the fight for social justice.

"The New Jim Crow" by Michelle Alexander - This book explores the ways in which the US criminal justice system perpetuates racial inequality through mass incarceration.

"Stamped from the Beginning" by Ibram X. Kendi - This book traces the history of racist ideas in the US and their impact on society.

"The Color of Law" by Richard Rothstein - This book reveals how government policies deliberately segregated African Americans in housing and created persistent racial inequities.

"Why Are All the Black Kids Sitting Together in the Cafeteria?" by Beverly Daniel Tatum - This book explores the psychological impact of racism and provides guidance for parents, educators, and community leaders to address racial issues.

"A People's History of the United States" by Howard Zinn - This book challenges traditional American history by centering marginalized and oppressed communities in the narrative.

"White Fragility" by Robin DiAngelo - This book examines the ways in which white people uphold racism and resist efforts to dismantle it.

"Slavery by Another Name" by Douglas A. Blackmon - This book exposes the use of forced labor in the US after the abolition of slavery and its long-lasting impact.

"The Warmth of Other Suns" by Isabel Wilkerson - This book tells the story of the Great Migration, in which millions of African Americans fled the Jim Crow South to the North and West.

"The Souls of Black Folk" by W.E.B. Du Bois - This classic work of African American literature explores the psychological impact of racism and the struggle for racial equality.

"Caste" by Isabel Wilkerson - This book examines the ways in which caste systems have been used to maintain hierarchy and oppression, including in the US.

"The Condemnation of Blackness" by Khalil Gibran Muhammad - This book explores the origins of racial stereotypes and how they have been used to justify discrimination and violence against Black people.

"Lies My Teacher Told Me" by James W. Loewen - This book exposes the myths and distortions in traditional American history textbooks.

"The Fire Next Time" by James Baldwin - This book is a personal essay on race in America that explores the psychological toll of racism and the possibility of achieving racial justice.

"Between the World and Me" by Ta-Nehisi Coates - This book is a letter to the author's son about what it means to be Black in America and the history of racism in the US.

"The Half Has Never Been Told" by Edward E. Baptist - This book examines the role of slavery in the US economy and its impact on American capitalism.

"The Black and the Blue" by Matthew Horace - This book examines the systemic racism in American law enforcement and offers suggestions for reform.

"Medical Apartheid" by Harriet A. Washington - This book exposes the history of medical experimentation on African

Americans and its impact on modern medicine.

"The Warmth of Other Suns" by Isabel Wilkerson - This book tells the story of the Great Migration, in which millions of African Americans fled the Jim Crow South to the North and West.

"The Autobiography of Malcolm X" by Malcolm X - This book is a powerful memoir that traces the author's transformation from a criminal to a political leader and provides insight into the experiences of Black Muslims in America.

"Invisible Man" by Ralph Ellison - This classic novel explores the psychological impact of racism on a Black man and his search for identity in a society that refuses to see him.

Articles:

"The Case for Reparations" by Ta-Nehisi Coates in The Atlantic - This article argues that the legacy of slavery and discrimination in the United States justifies reparations for Black Americans.

Mack Graham

"How Redlining Segregated America" by Alana Semuels in The Atlantic - This article explains the practice of redlining, which systematically denied mortgages and other loans to Black Americans, perpetuating racial segregation and inequality.

"The Unequal Toll of Toxic Stress" by Olga Khazan in The Atlantic - This article explores the link between racism and chronic stress, which can lead to a range of negative health outcomes.

"The Racist Roots of American Policing: From Slave Patrols to Traffic Stops" by Kia Gregory in The Guardian - This article traces the history of policing in the United States and the ways in which it has been used to oppress people of color.

"The Long-Lasting Legacy of the Great Migration" by Isabel Wilkerson in The New York Times - This article explores the impact of the Great Migration on American society and the enduring effects of racism and segregation.

"How School Segregation Divides Ferguson -- And the United States" by Nikole Hannah-Jones in ProPublica - This article examines the segregation of schools in Ferguson, Missouri, and its broader implications for the United States.

"What Is Systemic Racism?" by Jeneé Osterheldt in The Boston Globe - This article defines systemic racism and its effects on people of color, including disparities in health, education, and the criminal justice system.

"The Other Housing Crisis: Finding Fairness in the Face of Evictions" by Matthew Desmond in The New York Times - This article explores the impact of eviction on low-income families and the role of race and poverty in the housing crisis.

"The Myth of the Welfare Queen" by Josh Levin in Slate - This article debunks the stereotype of the "welfare queen" and reveals its roots in racial and gender bias.

"Why So Many Black Americans Are Skeptical of Covid Vaccines" by Jamelle Bouie in The New York Times - This article examines the history of medical racism and its impact on Black Americans' trust in the healthcare system.

"The History of Racial Covenants and How They Led to Segregation" by Emily Badger in The New York Times - This article explains the history of racial covenants, which were legal agreements that prohibited Black people from buying or renting homes in certain neighborhoods.

"The Great Land Robbery" by Vann R. Newkirk II in The Atlantic - This article reveals how the US government systematically stole land from Black farmers and Indigenous people, perpetuating racial inequality in wealth and property ownership.

"The School to Prison Pipeline, Explained" by German Lopez in Vox - This article describes the ways in which the education and criminal justice systems are intertwined and how this leads to the disproportionate punishment and incarceration of people of color.

"How Segregation Persists in America" by Alvin Chang in Vox - This article uses data visualization to show how segregation persists in the United States and the consequences of this segregation.

"The Disturbing Resilience of Scientific Racism" by Adam Hochschild in The New Yorker - This article examines the history of scientific racism and its contemporary manifestations in the fields of genetics and neuroscience.

"Racial Disparities in Maternal Health: An American Crisis" by Elizabeth Dawes Gay in Harvard Public Health Magazine - This article explains the racial disparities in maternal health outcomes and how systemic racism perpetuates these disparities.

"How Urban Renewal Created an American Apartheid" by Robert K. Nelson in The Conversation - This article explores the impact of urban renewal on communities of color and how it contributed to the creation of American apartheid.

Mack Graham

"The Impact of Racism on Child and Adolescent Health" by Maria Trent and Sana A. Loue in Pediatrics - This article reviews the literature on the impact of racism on child and adolescent health, including mental health, physical health, and access to care.

"The Racist Housing Policies That Built Ferguson" by Tanvi Misra in CityLab - This article explains how racist housing policies, including redlining and exclusionary zoning, created the racial segregation and economic disparities that exist in Ferguson, Missouri.

"The Racism We All Carry" by Barbara J. King in National Geographic - This article examines the ways in which unconscious bias and systemic racism are pervasive in society and how we can work to overcome them.

"The Death Gap" by David A. Ansell in The New Press - This article explores the racial disparities in health outcomes in the United States, and the role of systemic oppression in creating these disparities.

"The Great American Housing Bubble" by Devin Michelle Bunten in Current Affairs - This article examines the role of racial discrimination in the 2008 housing crisis and the ongoing legacy of segregation and inequality in American housing.

Deepening Your Understanding: 22 Online Courses, Workshops, and Seminars Led by Experts

Online Courses:

"Introduction to Social Justice" on Coursera - led by Professor Martha E. Gimenez. This course provides an introduction to social justice issues and explores key concepts such as equality, equity, and power.

"Racial Equity and the Science of Implicit Bias" on edX - led by Dr. John Dovidio and Dr. Patricia Devine. This course examines the science behind implicit bias and its role in perpetuating racial disparities in society.

"Social Justice and the City" on edX - led by Dr. Matthew Gandy. This course explores the ways in which urban spaces can be sites of both oppression and resistance, and examines strategies for achieving greater social justice in cities.

"Justice" on Harvard Online - led by Professor Michael Sandel. This course explores key ethical and moral questions related to justice, such as the role of punishment, the distribution of resources, and the limits of individual liberty.

"Criminal Justice Reform" on Coursera - led by Professor Phillip Atiba Goff. This course examines the problems with the criminal justice system in the United States and explores potential solutions for reform.

"Race and Cultural Diversity in American Life and History" on edX - led by Dr. George J. Sánchez. This course provides a historical overview of race and diversity in American society and explores the ways in which these issues continue to shape our world today.

"Human Rights: The Rights of Refugees" on edX - led by Professor Jacqueline Bhabha. This course examines the challenges faced by refugees and the legal and ethical frameworks that exist to protect their rights.

"Introduction to Women's and Gender Studies" on Coursera - led by Professor Jennifer Michelle Nash. This course provides an introduction to key concepts and debates in the field of women's and gender studies.

"Foundations of Positive Psychology" on Coursera - led by Professor Martin E.P. Seligman. This course explores the science of positive psychology, including topics such as happiness, well-being, and resilience.

"Social Justice in Public Health" on Coursera - led by Professor Jennifer K. Ibrahim. This course examines the relationship between public health and social justice, and explores strategies for promoting health equity.

"The Ethics of Memory" on edX - led by Dr. Jeffrey Olick. This course explores the ethical dimensions of memory, including questions of justice, responsibility, and historical trauma.

"The Psychology of Political Activism" on Coursera - led by Professor Gail L. Ferguson. This course explores the psychological and social factors that motivate political activism and social change.

"Global Justice" on edX - led by Professor Matthew Adler. This course explores key debates and theories related to global justice, including topics such as poverty, inequality, and climate change.

"Disability and Global Health" on Coursera - led by Professor Sofia Gruskin. This course examines the ways in which disability intersects with global health issues, including access to healthcare, poverty, and human rights.

"Environmental Justice" on Coursera - led by Professor Steve Wing. This course explores the ways in which environmental hazards and pollution disproportionately affect marginalized communities, and examines strategies for achieving greater environmental justice.

"Contemporary India: A Political and Social Overview" on edX - led by Professor Pratap Bhanu Mehta. This course provides an overview of contemporary Indian society and politics, including issues such as caste, gender, and globalization.

"Reparations and Racial Justice" on Coursera - led by Professor Michael Dawson. This course explores the history and contemporary relevance of reparations for historical injustices, with a focus on the case of African Americans in the United States.

"Critical Race Theory" on edX - led by Dr. Stephanie M. Wildman. This course provides an introduction to critical race theory, a framework for understanding how race intersects with systems of power and privilege.

"Leadership for Social Justice" on Coursera - led by Professor Douglas A. Hicks. This course examines the principles and practices of social justice leadership, and provides practical strategies for promoting equity and inclusion in various contexts.

"Indigenous Canada" on Coursera - led by Professor Tracy Bear. This course provides an overview of Indigenous history, culture, and contemporary issues in Canada, with a focus on decolonization and reconciliation.

"Black Lives Matter: From Hashtag to Movement" on edX - led by Dr. Keeanga-Yamahtta Taylor. This course explores the history and impact of the Black Lives Matter movement, and examines strategies for achieving racial justice and equity.

"LGBTQ Health" on Coursera - led by Professor Kenneth H. Mayer. This course examines the unique health issues faced by LGBTQ individuals, and explores strategies for promoting health equity and social justice for this population.

Workshops and Seminars:

"Anti-Racism 101" by Rachel Cargle - an introductory online course designed to provide participants with tools for identifying and addressing racism, offered on Rachel Cargle's website: rachelcargle.com.

"Abolitionist Teaching Network: Educators for Justice" by Dr. Bettina Love and others - a network of educators who aim to create a more equitable and just education system, with events and resources available

on their website:
abolitionistteachingnetwork.org.

"The Conscious Kid: Anti-Racism Education and Advocacy" by Dr. Erin Winkler and others - an online organization providing resources and workshops for parents and educators on raising and teaching anti-racist children, offered through their website: theconsciouskid.org.

"Intersectional Justice: Unpacking Race, Class, Gender and Sexuality" by Kimberlé Crenshaw and others - a webinar series exploring the intersectionality of social identities, offered by the African American Policy Forum on their website: aapf.org.

"Disability as Diversity: Implications for Social Justice" by Haben Girma - a webinar exploring the intersection of disability and social justice, offered through the Center for Education and Civil Rights at Penn State University on their website: ed.psu.edu/cecr.

"From Trauma to Trust: Reshaping Our Systems for Collective Well-Being" by Resmaa Menakem - an online workshop on addressing racial trauma and healing, offered by Resmaa Menakem on his website: resmaa.com.

"Mental Health and Wellness for Social Justice Advocates" by the National Queer and Trans Therapists of Color Network - a virtual event focusing on the mental health needs of social justice advocates, offered on their website: nqttcn.com.

"Indigenous Resistance in the 21st Century" by Nick Estes - a webinar on Indigenous activism and resistance, offered by Haymarket Books on their website: haymarketbooks.org.

"Decolonizing Wealth" by Edgar Villanueva - an online workshop on philanthropy and wealth redistribution, offered by Decolonizing Wealth Project on their website: decolonizingwealth.com.

"The Intersection of Immigration and Mass Incarceration" by Marielena Hincapié - a virtual event exploring the connections between immigration policy and mass incarceration, offered by the National

Immigration Law Center on their website: nilc.org.

"Introduction to Critical Race Theory" by Dr. Adrienne Keene - an online workshop introducing key concepts and debates in critical race theory, offered by Dr. Adrienne Keene on her website: nativeappropriations.com.

"Building Effective and Sustainable Anti-Racism Programs" by Dr. Derald Wing Sue - a virtual workshop providing guidance for organizations seeking to develop anti-racism programs, offered by Dr. Derald Wing Sue on his website: deraldsue.com.

"Queer and Trans Liberation" by Dean Spade - a webinar on the intersection of LGBTQ+ identities and social justice, offered by the Barnard Center for Research on Women on their website: bcrw.barnard.edu.

"Understanding and Addressing Islamophobia" by Dr. Khaled Beydoun - a virtual event exploring the roots and impact of Islamophobia, offered by the Arab

American National Museum on their website: arabamericanmuseum.org.

"Race, Gender, and the Fight for Voting Rights" by Carol Anderson - a webinar exploring the history of voting rights and its intersection with race and gender, offered by the University of Georgia on their website: uga.edu.

"Dismantling Anti-Blackness in Asian American Communities" by Cynthia Choi - a workshop exploring the history and impact of anti-Blackness in Asian American communities, offered by Asian Americans Advancing Justice on their website: advancingjustice-alc.org.

"Health Equity and Social Justice" by Dr. Camara Jones - an online course introducing key concepts and strategies for promoting health equity and social justice, offered by the Morehouse School of Medicine on their website: msm.edu.

"Environmental Justice and Climate Action" by Dr. Robert Bullard - a virtual event exploring the intersection of environmental justice and climate change, offered by the National Wildlife Federation on their website: nwf.org.

"Race, Gender, and Leadership in Social Justice Movements" by Dr. Dara Baldwin - a workshop exploring the dynamics of power and leadership in social justice movements, offered by the National Disability Rights Network on their website: ndrn.org.

"Gender-Based Violence and Social Justice" by Dr. Jackson Katz - an online course on addressing gender-based violence through a social justice lens, offered by Mentors in Violence Prevention on their website: mentorsinviolenceprevention.com.

"Racial Justice and Equity in Higher Education" by Dr. Shaun Harper - a virtual event exploring the history and current state of racial justice and equity in higher education, offered by the University of Southern California on their website: usc.edu.

"Queer Liberation and Social Justice" by Dean Spade - a webinar series exploring the intersection of queer identities and social

justice issues, offered by the Sylvia Rivera
Law Project on their website: srlp.org.

Fighting for Justice and Equity: 50 Inspiring Community-Led Organizations and Initiatives

The Gathering for Justice - The Gathering for Justice works to empower and amplify the voices of young people of color in the fight for social justice and human rights. - gatheringforjustice.org

Until Freedom - Until Freedom is an intersectional social justice organization that addresses systemic and structural racism, police brutality, and mass incarceration, and works to promote human rights and social justice for all. - untilfreedom.com

Youth Over Guns - Youth Over Guns is a youth-led organization that works to end gun violence and promote peace through policy change, community engagement, and public education. - youthoverguns.org

NNLB United - NNLB United is a non-profit organization that works to end gun violence and promote social justice in low-income communities through community organizing, youth empowerment, and policy advocacy. - nnlbunited.org

GoodCall NYC - GoodCall NYC is a grassroots organization based in Brooklyn that supports communities of color by providing free tax preparation, financial education, and legal services. goodcall.org

Black Lives Matter - Black Lives Matter is a global organization that advocates for an end to police brutality and promotes social, economic, and political justice for Black people. - blacklivesmatter.com

Color of Change - Color of Change is a non-profit organization that works to build power for Black communities and promote racial justice through online campaigns and grassroots organizing. - colorofchange.org

The Movement for Black Lives - The Movement for Black Lives is a coalition of organizations working to promote the dignity and rights of Black people through policy change, direct action, and public education. - m4bl.org

The NAACP - The National Association for the Advancement of Colored People (NAACP) is a historic civil rights organization that works to ensure political, educational, social, and economic equality for all people. - naacp.org

Southern Poverty Law Center - The Southern Poverty Law Center is a non-profit organization that fights hate and extremism through legal action, education, and advocacy. - splcenter.org

Showing Up for Racial Justice - Showing Up for Racial Justice is a national network of activists and organizers working to dismantle white supremacy and fight for racial justice. - showingupforracialjustice.org

The Equal Justice Initiative - The Equal Justice Initiative is a non-profit organization that works to end mass incarceration, challenge racial and economic injustice, and protect human rights for all. - eji.org

The ACLU - The American Civil Liberties Union (ACLU) works to protect and expand the rights and liberties guaranteed by the

Constitution and laws of the United States. - aclu.org

Muslim Advocates - Muslim Advocates is a national legal advocacy and educational organization that works to promote justice and equality for all, including Muslims and those affected by anti-Muslim bigotry. - muslimadvocates.org

United We Dream - United We Dream is the largest immigrant youth-led organization in the United States, working to promote the rights of immigrant communities and fight for social justice. - unitedwedream.org

National Domestic Workers Alliance - The National Domestic Workers Alliance is an organization that fights for the rights and dignity of domestic workers, including nannies, caregivers, and housecleaners. - domesticworkers.org

Indigenous Environmental Network - The Indigenous Environmental Network works to protect Indigenous lands, cultures, and communities from the impacts of climate change and environmental destruction. - ienearth.org

National LGBTQ Task Force - The National LGBTQ Task Force works to build power and promote equality for LGBTQ+ communities through grassroots organizing, policy advocacy, and public education. - thetaskforce.org

National Network for Immigrant and Refugee Rights - The National Network for Immigrant and Refugee Rights is an alliance of community-based organizations that works to protect the rights and dignity of immigrants and refugees. - nnirr.org

National Women's Law Center - The National Women's Law Center works to promote gender justice and equality through legal advocacy, public policy, and public education. - nwlc.org

National Urban League - The National Urban League is a civil rights organization that works to promote economic and social justice for African Americans and other underserved - nul.org communities.

National Council of La Raza - The National Council of La Raza is the largest national Hispanic civil rights and advocacy organization in the United States, working to promote social, economic, and political justice for Latino communities. - unidosus.org

Disability Rights Education and Defense Fund - The Disability Rights Education and Defense Fund is a leading disability rights legal and advocacy organization, working to protect and advance the rights of people with disabilities. - dredf.org

Race Forward - Race Forward is a non-profit organization that works to promote racial justice and equity through research, policy advocacy, and public education. - raceforward.org

The Transgender Law Center - The Transgender Law Center is the largest national trans-led organization advocating for the rights of transgender and gender nonconforming people, working to promote social justice and equity for all. - transgenderlawcenter.org

Mack Graham

The People's Budget LA - The People's Budget LA is a grassroots campaign led by Black Lives Matter and other community organizations that advocates for defunding the police and reinvesting in social programs and community-led initiatives. - peoplesbudgetla.com

Project NIA - Project NIA is a Chicago-based non-profit organization that works to end youth incarceration and promote community-based alternatives to youth justice. - project-nia.org

Street Roots - Street Roots is a newspaper and advocacy organization in Portland, Oregon, that works to end homelessness and poverty through grassroots organizing and public education.

Community Justice Project - The Community Justice Project is a Miami-based legal advocacy organization that works to promote racial justice and economic equity through litigation, policy advocacy, and community organizing. - communityjusticeproject.com

Detroit Justice Center - The Detroit Justice Center is a non-profit organization that works to promote social justice and equity in Detroit through legal services, community organizing, and public education. - detroitjustice.org

Dream Defenders - Dream Defenders is a youth-led organization that works to end systemic racism and promote social justice through grassroots organizing and direct action. - dreamdefenders.org

Grassroots Global Justice Alliance - The Grassroots Global Justice Alliance is a national network of grassroots organizations working to promote social and environmental justice through community organizing and advocacy. - grassrootsglobaljustice.org

Black Voters Matter - Black Voters Matter is a non-profit organization that works to increase political power and voter engagement in Black communities, and promote social and economic justice. - blackvotersmatterfund.org

The Laundromat Project - The Laundromat Project is a New York City-based non-profit organization that uses community art programs to promote social and racial justice. - laundromatproject.org

The International Indigenous Youth Council - The International Indigenous Youth Council is a youth-led organization that works to promote indigenous sovereignty and environmental justice through activism and community organizing. - indigenousyouth.org

The Advancement Project - The Advancement Project is a multi-racial civil rights organization that works to promote social and racial justice through litigation, policy advocacy, and community organizing. - advancementproject.org

Freedom, Inc. - Freedom, Inc. is a non-profit organization in Madison, Wisconsin, that works to promote social justice and equity through community organizing and advocacy. - freedom-inc.org

Take Back the Land - Take Back the Land is a national movement that works to end homelessness and promote housing justice through community organizing and direct action. - takebacktheland.org

The Poor People's Campaign - The Poor People's Campaign is a national movement that works to end poverty and promote economic and social justice through direct action, community organizing, and public education. - poorpeoplescampaign.org

Community Voices Heard - Community Voices Heard is a New York-based grassroots organization that works to promote social and economic justice through community organizing and public education. - cvhaction.org

Southerners on New Ground - Southerners on New Ground is a non-profit organization that works to promote LGBTQ+ rights, racial justice, and social and economic equity through community organizing and advocacy. - southernersonnewground.org

Critical Resistance - Critical Resistance is a national movement that works to end the prison-industrial complex and promote community-based alternatives to incarceration. - criticalresistance.org

Stop LAPD Spying Coalition - The Stop LAPD Spying Coalition is a Los Angeles-based community organization that works to end police surveillance and promote civil liberties and privacy rights. - stoplapdspying.org

Cooperation Jackson - Cooperation Jackson is a cooperative economic organization in Jackson, Mississippi, that works to promote economic democracy and community-based solutions to social and economic inequality. - cooperationjackson.org

The Partnership for Southern Equity - The Partnership for Southern Equity is an Atlanta-based non-profit organization that works to promote racial equity and social justice through research, advocacy, and community organizing. - partnershipforsouthernequity.org

Sacramento Area Congregations Together - Sacramento Area Congregations Together is a multi-faith community organization that works to promote social and economic justice in the Sacramento region through community organizing and advocacy. - sacramentact.org

SONG - SONG (Southerners on New Ground) is a regional organization that works to promote LGBTQ+ rights and racial justice in the southern United States through community organizing and advocacy. - songmatters.org

The Chicago Torture Justice Center - The Chicago Torture Justice Center is a non-profit organization that works to support survivors of police torture and promote reparations and justice for victims of police violence in Chicago. - chicagotorturejustice.org

Detroit Black Community Food Security Network - The Detroit Black Community Food Security Network is a non-profit organization that works to promote food justice and community-based solutions to food insecurity and poverty in Detroit. - detroitblackfoodsecurity.org

The Ella Baker Center for Human Rights - The Ella Baker Center for Human Rights is a

Mack Graham

non-profit organization based in Oakland, California, that works to promote racial and economic justice, and end mass incarceration through community organizing and advocacy. - ellabakercenter.org

Taking Action: 22 Guides for Building a More Just and Equitable Society

"The 10-Step Guide to Equity and Inclusion" by Nonprofit AF - This guide offers practical steps and strategies for organizations and individuals to promote equity and inclusion in their work and communities. - nonprofitaf.com

"5 Ways to Make Your Activism More Effective" by Teen Vogue - This guide offers tips and insights on how to make your activism more impactful and effective, including building coalitions, engaging with policymakers, and using social media. - teenvogue.com

"The People's Institute for Survival and Beyond Anti-Racism Principles" - This guide outlines anti-racism principles and strategies for individuals and organizations to promote racial equity and social justice. - thepeoplesinstitute.org

"Anti-Oppression Resource and Training Alliance Toolkit" - This toolkit offers resources and training materials for organizations and individuals to develop anti-oppression practices and strategies. - aorta.coop

"Queer and Trans Resistance: A Toolkit for Liberation" by the Sylvia Rivera Law Project - This guide offers tools and resources for queer and trans individuals and communities to resist oppression and promote liberation. - srlp.org

"The Activist's Toolkit" by Amnesty International - This toolkit offers resources and guidance for activists to take action on human rights issues, including advocacy, campaigning, and community organizing. - amnesty.org

"The Disability Justice Culture Club Resource List" - This comprehensive resource list provides information and tools for promoting disability justice and inclusion in various contexts, including education, activism, and media. - djcultureclub.wordpress.com

"Building Equitable Communities: A Guide to Community Development" by PolicyLink

- This guide offers a framework and strategies for building equitable and inclusive communities, including strategies for community engagement, economic development, and affordable housing. - policylink.org

"How to Build a Racially Diverse and Inclusive Nonprofit Board" by Candid - This guide offers tips and best practices for building a diverse and inclusive nonprofit board, including recruitment strategies and inclusive governance practices. - candid.org

"The Intersectionality Scorecard: A Tool for Gender and Racial Justice" by The Gender Equity and Racial Justice team at Change Elemental - This guide offers a tool for assessing and improving intersectionality and gender equity in organizations and communities. - changeelemental.org

"The White Accomplices Guide" by Showing Up for Racial Justice - This guide offers tips and resources for white people to be better accomplices in the fight for racial justice and equity. - showingupforracialjustice.org

Mack Graham

"The Feminist Guide to Policy Change" by the Global Network of Women Peacebuilders - This guide offers a framework and strategies for promoting feminist policy change in various contexts, including peacebuilding, security, and human rights. - gnwp.org

"Indigenous Ally Toolkit" by the Native Women's Association of Canada - This guide offers tools and resources for non-Indigenous individuals and communities to become better allies to Indigenous peoples and communities. - nwac.ca

"The Queer Justice League Toolkit" by the National Queer Asian Pacific Islander Alliance - This toolkit offers resources and guidance for individuals and organizations to promote LGBTQ+ rights and justice, including community organizing and advocacy. - nqapia.org

"Transformative Justice in Action" by Generation Five - This guide offers a framework and strategies for implementing transformative justice practices in various contexts, including addressing harm, building community, and promoting healing. - generationfive.org

"The Equity Audit: A Guide to Addressing Bias and Inequity in Schools" by Edutopia - This guide offers a framework and strategies for conducting an equity audit in schools to address bias and inequity in various areas, including curriculum, discipline, and hiring practices. - edutopia.org

"The Citizen's Guide to Climate Success" by Mark Jaccard - This guide offers insights and strategies for individuals and communities to take action on climate change, including policy advocacy and lifestyle changes. - citizensclimatelobby.org

"The Comprehensive Guide to Effective Giving" by The Life You Can Save - This guide offers resources and guidance for individuals to make effective and impactful donations to social justice causes and organizations. - thelifeyoucansave.org

"Know Your Rights: A Guide for Transgender and Gender Nonconforming Students" by Lambda Legal - This guide

144

offers information and resources for transgender and gender nonconforming students to understand their legal rights and navigate discrimination and harassment in school settings. - lambdalegal.org

"The Undocumented Student's Guide to College" by The Best Colleges - This guide offers information and resources for undocumented students to navigate the college application process and access financial aid and scholarships. - thebestcolleges.org

"Self-Care Tips for Black People Who Are Struggling with This Very Painful Week" by Black Lives Matter - This guide offers self-care tips and resources for Black people to cope with the effects of systemic racism and violence, particularly during times of crisis and trauma. - blacklivesmatter.com

"A Guide to Muslim Women's Rights" by the Council on American-Islamic Relations - This guide offers information and resources for Muslim women to understand their legal rights and navigate discrimination and harassment in various settings, including the workplace and schools. - cair.com

"The Indigenous Peoples' Guide to Arctic Refuge Defense" by the Gwich'in Steering Committee - This guide offers information and resources for Indigenous peoples to advocate for the protection of the Arctic National Wildlife Refuge, a sacred site for the Gwich'in people, and to resist extractive industries that threaten their land and culture. - ourarcticrefuge.org

Empowering Your Advocacy: 36 Online Tools and Resources for Activism and Advocacy

ActBlue - a platform for donating to Democratic candidates and progressive causes - actblue.com

Action Network - a platform for creating and joining advocacy campaigns on various issues - actionnetwork.org

Amnesty Decoders - a tool for analyzing satellite images to identify and document human rights abuses - amnesty.org

Avaaz - a global platform for taking action on a range of issues, including climate change, human rights, and economic justice - avaaz.org

Be My Eyes - an app that connects sighted volunteers with blind or visually impaired people who need assistance - bemyeyes.com

Black Lives Matter - a movement for racial justice and ending police brutality - blacklivesmatter.com

Change.org - a platform for creating and signing petitions on a variety of social justice issues - change.org

ColorLines - a news and analysis site that centers on the perspectives and experiences of people of color - colorlines.com

Courage to Resist - a platform for supporting U.S. military war resisters and conscientious objectors - couragetoresist.org

Countable - a tool for tracking legislation and contacting elected officials - countable.us

Credo Action - a platform for taking action on a variety of social justice issues - credoaction.com

Daily Action - a tool for receiving daily actions to take on various political and

social issues via text message -
dailyaction.org

Demand Progress - a platform for
advocating for progressive policies on issues
such as internet freedom and government
transparency - demandprogress.org

DREAM Act Toolkit - a resource for
advocating for immigrant rights and the
DREAM Act - unitedwedream.org

Everytown for Gun Safety - a platform for
advocating for gun safety laws and policies -
everytown.org
Fight for $15 - a movement for raising the
minimum wage to $15 per hour -
fightfor15.org

Fight for the Future - a platform for
advocating for internet freedom and privacy
- fightforthefuture.org

Future Majority - a platform for mobilizing
young voters and advocating for
progressive policies - futuremajority.org

Global Citizen - a platform for taking action on global poverty, health, and environmental issues - globalcitizen.org

Good Call - a tool for connecting people in police custody with free legal support - goodcall.org

Grist - a news and analysis site that focuses on climate and environmental issues - grist.org

iNaturalist - a tool for recording and sharing observations of biodiversity - inaturalist.org

Indivisible - a network of local grassroots groups organizing for progressive policies and candidates - indivisible.org

Justia - a legal research site that provides free access to case law, statutes, and legal resources - justia.com

MapLight - a platform for tracking money in politics and government - maplight.org

MoveOn.org - a platform for organizing and mobilizing on progressive issues - moveon.org

Mack Graham

Resistbot - a tool for contacting elected officials via text message - resist.bot

Save the Internet - a platform for advocating for net neutrality and an open internet - savetheinternet.com

The Trevor Project - a platform for providing crisis intervention and suicide prevention services to LGBTQ+ young people - thetrevorproject.org

Trans Lifeline - a crisis hotline for transgender people, staffed by transgender people - translifeline.org

TurboVote - a tool for registering to vote and receiving election reminders - turbovote.org

Ultraviolet - a platform for taking action on issues affecting women, including reproductive rights, economic justice, and ending gender-based violence - weareultraviolet.org

United States Holocaust Memorial Museum - a platform for education, remembrance, and advocacy on issues related to the Holocaust and genocide - ushmm.org

Vote.org - a tool for checking voter registration status, registering to vote, and finding polling locations - vote.org

#VOTEPROCHOICE - a platform for connecting voters with pro-choice candidates and resources - voteprochoice.us

Vote Riders - a platform for promoting voter ID education and assistance to ensure that all eligible voters can cast their ballots - voteriders.org

Self-Care for Hope Dealerz: 12 Essential Guides and Mental Health Hotlines

Guides:

"Self-Care for People of Color After Psychological Trauma" by the American Psychological Association - www.apa.org

"Self-Care for Activists" by The University of California, Berkeley - uhs.berkeley.edu

"10 Self-Care Strategies for Activists" by Everyday Feminism - everydayfeminism.com

"Self-Care for Social Justice Activists" by GoodTherapy - www.goodtherapy.org

"The Activist's Guide to Mental Health" by The Mighty - themighty.com

"12 Ways to Practice Self-Care in the Age of Trump" by Teen Vogue - www.teenvogue.com

"10 Simple Self-Care Tips for Activists" by The Tempest - thetempest.co

"A Toolkit for Self-Care in Activist Work" by School of Social Work, University of Michigan - ssw.umich.edu

"Mental Health and Self-Care for Activists" by ACLU - www.aclu.org

"Self-Care Tips for Social Justice Advocates" by Our Bodies Ourselves - www.ourbodiesourselves.org

"6 Ways for Activists to Practice Self-Care and Avoid Burnout" by NBC News - www.nbcnews.com

"Self-Care for the Socially Conscious" by Lifehacker - lifehacker.com

Mental Health Hotlines:

National Suicide Prevention Lifeline: 1-800-273-8255 - A 24/7 hotline for people in distress or crisis who may be experiencing suicidal thoughts or feelings.

Mack Graham

Crisis Text Line: Text HOME to 741741 - A free, 24/7 text message-based support line for people in crisis.

The Trevor Project: 1-866-488-7386 - A 24/7 crisis intervention and suicide prevention hotline for LGBTQ+ youth.

National Domestic Violence Hotline: 1-800-799-7233 - A 24/7 hotline for people experiencing domestic violence or abuse.

Disaster Distress Helpline: 1-800-985-5990 - A 24/7 hotline for people experiencing emotional distress related to natural or human-caused disasters.

National Alliance on Mental Illness (NAMI) Helpline: 1-800-950-NAMI (6264) - A hotline for information and support related to mental health conditions.

SAMHSA National Helpline: 1-800-662-HELP (4357) - A confidential, free, 24/7 hotline for people experiencing mental health or substance abuse issues.

RAINN (Rape, Abuse, and Incest National Network) Hotline: 1-800-656-HOPE (4673) -

A 24/7 hotline for people who have experienced sexual assault or abuse.

Trans Lifeline: 1-877-565-8860 - A hotline for transgender people in crisis or distress.

Substance Abuse and Mental Health Services Administration (SAMHSA) Disaster Distress Helpline: 1-800-985-5990 - A 24/7 hotline for people experiencing emotional distress related to disasters.

Veterans Crisis Line: 1-800-273-8255, Press 1 - A confidential, toll-free hotline for veterans and their families experiencing emotional distress or crises.

Eating Disorders Helpline: 1-800-931-2237 - A hotline for information and support related to eating disorders.

LGBTQ National Hotline: 1-888-843-4564 - A hotline providing confidential support for LGBTQ individuals, staffed by LGBTQ volunteers.

Please note that these hotlines are based in the United States and may not be available in all countries.

Finding Calm: 12 Mindfulness Apps for Reducing Stress in Your Daily Life

Headspace - Offers guided meditations and mindfulness exercises for a range of topics and situations.

Calm - Provides guided meditations, breathing exercises, and sleep stories to reduce stress and improve well-being.

Insight Timer - Offers a variety of guided meditations, music, and talks from experts in the field.

10% Happier - Provides guided meditations and courses on mindfulness and meditation, with a focus on reducing anxiety and stress.

Stop, Breathe & Think - Offers guided meditations tailored to the user's emotions and mood, as well as breathing exercises and mindfulness practices.

Smiling Mind - Provides mindfulness and meditation exercises for all ages, with a focus on reducing stress and improving overall well-being.

Mindbody - Offers guided meditations, yoga classes, and other wellness practices to promote mindfulness and relaxation.

The Mindfulness App - Provides guided meditations and mindfulness exercises for stress reduction and personal growth.

Aura - Offers personalized mindfulness meditations and tracks user's mood and stress levels to tailor mindfulness practices to the individual.

Simple Habit - Provides guided meditations and courses tailored to specific needs, such as anxiety, sleep, and stress management.

Breethe - Offers guided meditations, breathing exercises, and sleep stories for relaxation and mindfulness.

Oak - Provides guided meditations and breathing exercises for relaxation, focus, and sleep.

Amplifying Our Voices: 40 Powerful Podcasts Exploring Social Justice Issues

Earn Your Leisure – Focus on financial literacy and building generational wealth, featuring guests from diverse backgrounds who have achieved success in business and entrepreneurship

Street Politicians - a podcast on politics, social justice, and culture.

Code Switch - Examines issues of race and identity in America.

The Stoop - Explores stories from across the Black diaspora.

1619 - A New York Times podcast that examines the legacy of slavery in America.

Black Wall Street Today - a podcast on Black entrepreneurship and economic development.

Do The Work - a podcast on social justice issues.

Latino USA - Covers news and issues of importance to the Latinx community in the United States.

The Nod - Explores Black culture and experiences.

The Daily from The New York Times - Covers a range of news and issues, often including social justice topics.

The United States of Anxiety - Focuses on political and social issues in America.

Still Processing - Explores culture and politics in America from the perspective of two Black, queer hosts.

The Guilty Feminist - Examines feminism and social justice issues from a humorous perspective.

The Queer Arabs - Explores the experiences and perspectives of queer Arabs.

Reveal - A podcast that focuses on investigative journalism and social justice issues.

Mack Graham

Ear Hustle - Takes listeners inside the prison system to explore the experiences of incarcerated people.

You Had Me at Black - Shares stories and experiences of Black people in America.

The Color Line Murders - Examines the unsolved murders of Black people in America.

Pod Save the People - Hosted by organizer and activist DeRay Mckesson, covers news and issues related to social justice.

Latinos Out Loud - Explores issues of importance to the Latinx community in a humorous and irreverent way.

Black Wall Street 1921 - Examines the history of the Tulsa Race Massacre.

On Being with Krista Tippett - Explores issues of spirituality, social justice, and the human experience.

Throughline - A podcast that examines history to shed light on current events and social issues.

Intersectionality Matters! - Hosted by Kimberlé Crenshaw, a podcast that explores intersectionality and social justice issues.

Our Body Politic - Covers news and politics from the perspective of women of color.

Democracy Now! - A news program that covers a range of social justice issues from a progressive perspective.

Latinos Who Lunch - Two friends talk about art, food, and culture from a Latinx perspective.

The Secret Lives of Black Women - Hosted by two Black women, the podcast covers a range of topics related to Black women's experiences.

All My Relations - A podcast that explores the relationships between Native people and their communities, and the land they inhabit.

The Breakdown with Shaun King - A podcast that covers current events from a social justice perspective.

The Ezra Klein Show - A podcast that features in-depth conversations with guests on politics, media, and society.

The Brown Liquor Report - A podcast that covers politics, pop culture, and social issues from a Black perspective.

Good Ancestor Podcast - Hosted by author and speaker Layla F. Saad, this podcast explores topics related to race, identity, and social justice.

The Way We Live Now - A podcast that explores the intersection of COVID-19 and social justice issues.

Queerology - A podcast that explores the intersections of faith and queer identity.

Still Processing - A culture podcast that explores the intersection of art, politics, and society.

Hoodrat to Headwrap - A podcast that explores Black feminist theory and the experiences of Black women.

The Intercept - A podcast that covers politics, social justice issues, and investigative journalism.

Groundings - A podcast that explores the intersection of Black culture, politics, and social issues.

19 Keys - A podcast that explores various topics related to personal development, financial literacy, and building generational wealth, with a focus on empowering marginalized communities

Inclusive Leadership: 20 Resources for Developing Strong and Inclusive Leadership Skills

The Leadership Challenge - A program that teaches leadership skills through training, coaching, and development tools. - leadershipchallenge.com

Center for Creative Leadership - Offers leadership development programs, workshops, and assessments for individuals and organizations. - ccl.org

Harvard Kennedy School Executive Education - Offers a variety of leadership development programs for individuals and organizations. - hks.harvard.edu/executive-education

Emerging Leaders Program - A program that provides mentorship and training for young professionals looking to develop their leadership skills. - acg.org/global/programs/emerging-leaders-program

The Aspen Institute - Provides leadership development programs for individuals and organizations with a focus on social impact. - aspeninstitute.org

Management Leadership for Tomorrow - Provides career development and leadership training for underrepresented minorities. - ml4t.org

The Global Leadership Network - Offers leadership training and development programs for individuals and organizations. - globalleadership.org

The Center for Nonprofit Management - Offers leadership development programs for nonprofit organizations and their staff. - cnm.org

Women's Leadership Institute - Provides leadership training and development for women in various industries. - wliut.com

Leadership Austin - Provides leadership training and development for individuals and organizations in the Austin, Texas area. - leadershipaustin.org

Leadership Greater Chicago - Provides leadership development programs for individuals and organizations in the Chicago area. - lgcchicago.org

Rockwood Leadership Institute - Provides leadership development programs for social change leaders. - rockwoodleadership.org

The Coaches Training Institute - Offers leadership coaching and training for individuals and organizations. - coactive.com

The Bridgespan Group - Offers leadership development programs and resources for nonprofit leaders. - bridgespan.org

LeaderShape - Provides leadership development programs and resources for college students and professionals. - leadershape.org

The Nonprofit Leadership Alliance - Offers leadership development programs and certifications for nonprofit professionals. - nonprofitleadershipalliance.org

The National Leadership Institute - Provides leadership development programs and resources for public safety professionals. - www.national-li.com

The Social Change Initiative - Provides leadership development programs and resources for social change leaders. - socialchangeinitiative.com

The OpEd Project - Offers training and coaching for individuals looking to develop their thought leadership skills. - theopedproject.org

The Mandela Washington Fellowship - Provides leadership training and development for young African leaders. - mandelawashingtonfellowship.org

Please note that some of these programs may have specific eligibility criteria and may require an application process.

Organizing and Advocacy: 33 Essential Resources for Empowering Communities

Grassroots Fundraising Journal - a quarterly publication that provides fundraising and organizing tips for nonprofit organizations and grassroots groups. Website: grassrootsfundraising.org

Nonprofit AF - a blog that provides resources and advice on nonprofit management and community organizing. Website: nonprofitaf.com

The Organizing Academy - a training program for organizers and activists on how to build power and mobilize communities. Website: organizingacademy.com

Community Tool Box - a free online resource for community organizers that provides guidance on various aspects of community development, including organizing, planning, and evaluation. Website: ctb.ku.edu

The Mobilization Lab - a resource hub for community organizers that provides training materials, guides, and case studies on organizing and mobilizing communities. Website: mobilisationlab.org

The Resistance Manual - a crowd-sourced online guide that provides information and resources on a variety of social justice issues and how to take action on them. Website: resistancemanual.org

Center for Community Change - an organization that provides resources and training to community organizers on how to build power and create change at the local, state, and national levels. Website: communitychange.org

The People's Lobby - an organization that provides resources and training for community organizers on issues such as economic justice, environmental justice, and immigrant rights. Website: thepeopleslobbyusa.org

Movement Strategy Center - an organization that provides resources and training for community organizers on how

to build powerful social movements.
Website: movementstrategy.org

Campaign Bootcamp - a training program
for community organizers and activists on
how to run effective campaigns and create
change. Website: campaignbootcamp.org

Midwest Academy - a training institute for
community organizers and activists on how
to build power and create social change.
Website: midwestacademy.com

Social Movement Technologies - a resource
hub for community organizers that provides
training materials, guides, and tools on
organizing and mobilizing communities.
Website: socialmovementtechnologies.org

SmartMeme - an organization that provides
resources and training for community
organizers on how to use strategic
storytelling and narrative to create social
change. Website: smartmeme.org

Blueprint for Social Justice - a guide to
community organizing and strategic
planning, developed by the Center for Social

Inclusion. Website:
centerforsocialinclusion.org

Organize Training Center - a training
institute for community organizers and
activists on how to build power and create
social change. Website:
organizetrainingcenter.org

Citizen Engagement Laboratory - an
organization that provides resources and
training for community organizers on how
to use digital tools and technology to create
social change. Website:
citizenengagementlab.org

Alliance for Justice - an organization that
provides resources and training for
community organizers and nonprofits on
how to engage in advocacy and lobbying.
Website: afj.org

The Participatory Budgeting Project - an
organization that provides resources and
training for community organizers on how
to implement participatory budgeting, a
democratic process for allocating public
funds. Website: participatorybudgeting.org

Mack Graham

The Plan of Chicago - a guide to community organizing and planning, developed by the Chicago Metropolitan Agency for Planning. Website: cmap.illinois.gov

The Ruckus Society - an organization that provides resources and training for community organizers on how to use direct action and creative activism to create social change. Website: ruckus.org

Wellstone Action - an organization that provides resources and training for community organizers and activists on how to run effective political campaigns and create change. Website: wellstone.org

The Advocacy Institute - an organization that provides resources and training for community organizers on how to engage in effective advocacy and lobbying. Website: advocacy.org

The Center for Democracy and Citizenship - an organization that provides resources and training for community organizers and activists. Website: community-wealth.org/content/center-democracy-and-citizenship

Popular Resistance - A platform that provides news, analysis, and organizing resources to support social movements and political struggles. Website: popularresistance.org

Progressive Change Campaign Committee (PCCC) - A political action committee that supports progressive candidates and mobilizes grassroots campaigns for progressive causes. Website: boldprogressives.org

Public Citizen - An organization that advocates for consumer rights and government transparency and accountability, providing resources for grassroots organizing and campaigns. Website: citizen.org

Resource Generation - A group of young people with wealth who use their resources and privilege to support progressive social movements and promote economic justice. Website: resourcegeneration.org

School of Unity and Liberation (SOUL) - A center for training and supporting young

leaders in social justice organizing and
activism. Website: soulo.org

Showing Up for Racial Justice (SURJ) - A
national network of groups and individuals
working to undermine white supremacy
and promote racial justice. Website:
showingupforracialjustice.org

The Resistance Manual - An open-source
guide to understanding and taking action on
various political and social issues. Website:
theresistancemanual.org

United for a Fair Economy - An organization
that works to promote economic justice
and challenge economic inequality,
providing resources for community
organizing and advocacy. Website:
faireconomy.org

The Organizing Institute - provides training
and support for progressive organizers and
activists. Website:
theorganizinginstitute.com

MoveOn.org - provides resources and tools
for grassroots organizing and advocacy.
Website: front.moveon.org

Personal and Professional Development: 24 Educational Resources for Empowering Communities

Khan Academy - offers free online courses in a variety of subjects, including math, science, and humanities. Website: khanacademy.org

Codeacademy - offers interactive coding lessons in programming languages like Python, Java, and HTML/CSS. Website: codecademy.com

Udemy - offers affordable online courses in a range of subjects, from business and tech to personal development and the arts. Website: udemy.com

LinkedIn Learning - offers on-demand video courses taught by industry experts in a range of subjects, including business, creative, and technology. Website: linkedin.com/learning

Coursera - offers online courses and specializations from top universities in a variety of fields, from business and computer science to health and social sciences. Website: coursera.org

edX - offers free online courses from top universities in a variety of subjects, including computer science, business, and engineering. Website: edx.org

FutureLearn - offers free online courses and degrees from top universities and organizations in the UK and around the world. Website: futurelearn.com

MIT OpenCourseWare - offers free online access to course materials from thousands of MIT courses in a range of subjects, from architecture to economics. Website: ocw.mit.edu/index.htm

Harvard Online Learning - offers online courses, certificates, and degrees from Harvard University in a range of fields, including business, health, and law. Website: pll.harvard.edu

Open Yale Courses - offers free access to online courses taught by Yale professors in a variety of subjects, including psychology, philosophy, and literature. Website: oyc.yale.edu

FreeCodeCamp - offers free online courses and projects to help individuals learn web development skills, from HTML/CSS to full-stack development. Website: freecodecamp.org

The Odin Project - offers a free and open-source web development curriculum that covers topics like HTML/CSS, JavaScript, and Ruby on Rails. Website: theodinproject.com

Flatiron School - offers online and in-person courses in software engineering, data science, and cybersecurity. Website: flatironschool.com

General Assembly - offers courses and workshops in a range of fields, from data science and web development to product management and digital marketing. Website: generalassemb.ly

Harvard Business School Online - offers online courses and certificates in business topics like marketing, finance, and leadership. Website: online.hbs.edu

Lynda - offers on-demand video courses in a variety of subjects, from business and design to photography and software development. Website: lynda.com

Google Digital Garage - offers free online courses and tutorials in digital marketing, data analysis, and other tech-related skills. Website: learndigital.withgoogle.com/digitalgarage

Alison - offers free online courses and certifications in a range of subjects, from business and technology to health and humanities. Website: alison.com

Skillshare - offers online courses and workshops in creative fields like art, design, and photography. Website: skillshare.com

Treehouse - offers online courses in web development, mobile development, and game development. Website: teamtreehouse.com

DataCamp - offers online courses and projects in data science and analytics, from

Python and R to machine learning and data visualization. Website: datacamp.com

Pluralsight. Website: offers online courses in tech fields like software development, cybersecurity, and data science - pluralsight.com

MasterClass - An online learning platform featuring classes taught by world-renowned experts in fields such as cooking, writing, and music. Website: masterclass.com

Open Culture - A website offering free online courses, audio books, and other educational resources on a wide range of subjects. Website: openculture.com

Empowering Advocacy and Policy Change: 26 Essential Resources

Open Secrets - A nonpartisan organization that tracks money in politics and its effect on elections and public policy. Website: opensecrets.org

Ballotpedia - A comprehensive online encyclopedia of American politics and elections, including information on elected officials and upcoming elections. Website: ballotpedia.org

GovTrack - A website that tracks federal legislation and the voting records of elected officials. Website: govtrack.us

VoteSmart - A website that provides information on elected officials and candidates, including their voting records, campaign finance information, and issue positions. Website: votesmart.org

Sunlight Foundation - An organization that advocates for open government and

transparency in political decision-making.
Website: sunlightfoundation.com

Public Citizen - A nonprofit organization
that advocates for consumer rights and
government accountability. Website:
citizen.org

Common Cause - A nonprofit organization
that advocates for government
accountability and transparency, and works
to reduce the influence of money in politics.
Website: commoncause.org

Center for Public Integrity - A nonprofit
investigative journalism organization that
exposes abuses of power and government
corruption. Website: publicintegrity.org

Center for Responsive Politics - A
nonpartisan organization that tracks money
in politics and its influence on policy
decisions. Website: opensecrets.org

ProPublica - An investigative journalism
organization that produces in-depth
reporting on a range of issues, including
government corruption and abuse of
power. Website: propublica.org

National Priorities Project - A nonpartisan research organization that provides information on federal spending and its impact on public policy. Website: nationalpriorities.org

Project Vote Smart - A nonpartisan organization that provides information on elected officials and candidates, including their voting records and issue positions. Website: votesmart.org

American Civil Liberties Union (ACLU) - An organization that defends and preserves individual rights and liberties, including freedom of speech and equal protection under the law. Website: aclu.org

NAACP Legal Defense and Educational Fund - An organization that works to secure equal rights and justice for African Americans and other minorities. Website: naacpldf.org

Human Rights Campaign - An organization that advocates for LGBTQ+ rights and equality. Website: hrc.org

League of Women Voters - An organization that works to empower voters and defend democracy. Website: lwv.org

National Women's Law Center - An organization that advocates for women's rights and economic justice. Website: nwlc.org

Emily's List - An organization that works to elect pro-choice Democratic women to office. Website: emilyslist.org

National Council of La Raza - An organization that advocates for Hispanic Americans and works to advance their civil rights and economic opportunities. Website: nclr.org

National Immigration Forum - An organization that advocates for immigration reform and promotes the value of immigrants to America. Website: immigrationforum.org

Oxfam America - An organization that works to alleviate poverty and injustice around the world. Website: oxfamamerica.org

Bread for the World - A Christian organization that works to end hunger and poverty in the United States and around the world. Website: bread.org

American Association of People with Disabilities - An organization that advocates for the rights of people with disabilities and works to ensure their full inclusion in society. Website: aapd.com

National Alliance on Mental Illness (NAMI) - An organization that provides education and support to those affected by mental illness. Website: nami.org

Represent.us - a nonpartisan organization dedicated to ending political corruption and promoting government accountability through policy change and grassroots organizing. Website: represent.us

All On The Line - a campaign to end gerrymandering and ensure fair redistricting. Website: allontheline.org

Building Healthy Communities: 36 Resources for Physical and Mental Wellness

American Heart Association - a nonprofit organization that provides resources and information on heart health, healthy eating, and exercise. Website: heart.org

CDC Health Topics A to Z - a comprehensive list of health topics and resources provided by the Centers for Disease Control and Prevention (CDC) . Website: cdc.gov/az

Mental Health America - a nonprofit organization that provides information and resources on mental health, including support groups and online tools for mental health screening. Website: mhanational.org

Substance Abuse and Mental Health Services Administration (SAMHSA) - a government agency that provides information and resources on mental health and substance abuse, including a national helpline. Website: samhsa.gov

National Eating Disorders Association (NEDA) - a nonprofit organization that provides resources and support for individuals and families affected by eating disorders. Website: nationaleatingdisorders.org

National Institute of Mental Health (NIMH) - a government agency that provides information and resources on mental health research and treatment. Website: nimh.nih.gov

Healthfinder.gov - a government website that provides information and resources on a variety of health topics, including disease prevention and healthy living. Website: healthfinder.gov

The Health Gap - a nonprofit organization that works to address health disparities and promote health equity in Cincinnati, Ohio. Website: thehealthgap.org

National Institute on Drug Abuse (NIDA) - a government agency that provides information and resources on drug abuse and addiction, including a helpline and treatment locator. Website: drugabuse.gov

National Alliance for Hispanic Health - a nonprofit organization that provides resources and advocacy on health issues affecting Hispanic communities. Website: healthyamericas.org

Association of Asian Pacific Community Health Organizations (AAPCHO) - a nonprofit organization that advocates for and supports community health centers serving Asian Americans, Native Hawaiians, and Pacific Islanders. Website: aapcho.org

National Council of Urban Indian Health - a nonprofit organization that provides support and resources for urban Indian health centers and advocates for the health and wellness of urban Indigenous populations. Website: urbanindianhealth.org

Planned Parenthood - a nonprofit organization that provides reproductive healthcare services, including birth control, STI testing and treatment, and cancer screenings. Website: plannedparenthood.org

Health Resources and Services Administration (HRSA) - a government agency that provides funding and support for community health centers and other healthcare services in underserved areas. Website: hrsa.gov

Women's Health - a government website that provides information and resources on women's health issues, including reproductive health, pregnancy, and menopause. Website: womenshealth.gov

The Black Women's Health Imperative - a nonprofit organization that advocates for and provides resources on health issues affecting Black women and girls. Website: bwhi.org

American Diabetes Association - a nonprofit organization that provides resources and support for individuals and families affected by diabetes, including information on healthy living and managing diabetes. Website: diabetes.org

Center for Black Women's Wellness - a nonprofit organization that provides health education and support for Black women

and their families in Atlanta, Georgia.
Website: cbww.org

National Kidney Foundation - a nonprofit
organization that provides information and
resources on kidney health and disease
prevention. Website: kidney.org

**National LGBTQIA+ Health Education
Center** - a nonprofit organization that
provides training and resources on
LGBTQIA+ health issues for healthcare
providers and advocates for LGBTQIA+
health equity. Website:
lgbtqiahealtheducation.org

March of Dimes - a nonprofit organization
that works to improve maternal and infant
health outcomes, including research and
advocacy on preterm birth and birth
defects. Website: marchofdimes.org

**National Association of Community Health
Centers** - a nonprofit organization that
supports and advocates for community
health centers serving underserved and
vulnerable populations. Website: nachc.org

Mack Graham

American Sexual Health Association (ASHA) - A nonprofit organization that provides information and resources on sexual health and wellness, including STI prevention and treatment. Website: ashasexualhealth.org

National Council for Behavioral Health - A nonprofit organization that provides resources and advocacy on behavioral health issues, including mental health and addiction. Website: thenationalcouncil.org

American Foundation for Suicide Prevention (AFSP) - A nonprofit organization that provides information, resources, and support for people affected by suicide, including prevention and crisis intervention. Website: afsp.org

Center for Disease Control and Prevention (CDC) - A federal agency that provides information and resources on a wide range of health topics, including disease prevention, nutrition, and environmental health. Website: cdc.gov

Office of Disease Prevention and Health Promotion (ODPHP) - A federal agency that provides information and resources on disease prevention, health promotion, and healthy lifestyles. Website: health.gov/our-work/odphp

National Women's Health Network - A nonprofit organization that provides information, resources, and advocacy on women's health issues, including reproductive health, breastfeeding, and menopause. Website: nwhn.org

Men's Health Network - A nonprofit organization that provides information, resources, and advocacy on men's health issues, including prostate cancer, cardiovascular health, and mental health. Website: menshealthnetwork.org

American Heart Association (AHA) - A nonprofit organization that provides information and resources on heart health, including prevention and treatment of heart disease. Website: heart.org

American Diabetes Association (ADA) - A nonprofit organization that provides information and resources on diabetes prevention and management, including

healthy eating and physical activity.
Website: diabetes.org

National Multiple Sclerosis Society - A
nonprofit organization that provides
information, resources, and support for
people affected by multiple sclerosis,
including treatment options and advocacy
for research and policy change. Website:
nationalmssociety.org

Arthritis Foundation - A nonprofit
organization that provides information and
resources on arthritis prevention and
management, including healthy living
strategies and research updates. Website:
arthritis.org

American Lung Association - A nonprofit
organization that provides information and
resources on lung health, including
prevention and treatment of lung diseases
such as asthma and COPD. Website:
lung.org

National Sleep Foundation - A nonprofit
organization that provides information and
resources on sleep health, including tips for
healthy sleep habits and treatment options

for sleep disorders. Website: sleepfoundation.org

National Institute on Aging (NIA) - A government agency that provides information and resources on healthy aging, including exercise and nutrition tips and strategies for managing chronic conditions. Website: nia.nih.gov

Empowering Job Creation: 25 Resources for Starting and Growing Businesses and Accessing Financing

SCORE: A national nonprofit organization that offers free business mentoring, workshops, and resources for small business owners and entrepreneurs. Website: score.org

Small Business Administration (SBA): A U.S. government agency that provides resources, including loans and training programs, to help small businesses start, grow, and succeed. Website: sba.gov

Kauffman Foundation: A nonprofit organization that provides resources and support for entrepreneurs and small business owners. Website: kauffman.org

National Association of Small Business Owners (NASBO): An organization that provides resources, support, and advocacy for small business owners. Website: nasbo.org

National Minority Supplier Development Council (NMSDC): An organization that helps minority-owned businesses connect with corporate and government buyers. Website: nmsdc.org

Women's Business Centers: A network of centers across the U.S. that provide training, counseling, and resources for women entrepreneurs. Website: sba.gov/offices/womens-business-centers

Association for Enterprise Opportunity (AEO): An organization that provides resources and support for microbusinesses and small business owners. Website: aeoworks.org

Small Business Development Centers (SBDCs): A network of centers across the U.S. that provide free one-on-one business counseling, training, and resources for small business owners. Website: americassbdc.org

National Association for the Self-Employed (NASE): An organization that provides resources and support for self-employed individuals and microbusiness owners. Website: nase.org

National Business Incubation Association (NBIA): An organization that provides resources and support for business incubators and entrepreneurship programs. Website: inbia.org

Women's Economic Ventures: A nonprofit organization that provides training, loans, and other resources to help women start and grow businesses. Website: wevonline.org

Minority Business Development Agency (MBDA): A U.S. government agency that provides resources and support for minority-owned businesses. Website: mbda.gov

National Association of Women Business Owners (NAWBO): An organization that provides resources, support, and advocacy for women business owners. Website: nawbo.org

Association of Women's Business Centers: A network of centers across the U.S. that provides training, counseling, and resources for women entrepreneurs. Website: awbc.org

National Urban League Entrepreneurship Center: A program that provides resources and support for entrepreneurs in urban communities. Website: nulec.org

Minority Finance Forum: An organization that provides resources and support for minority-owned businesses in the finance industry. Website: minorityfinance.com

Association for Corporate Growth (ACG): An organization that provides resources and support for middle-market businesses and investors. Website: acg.org

Community Development Financial Institutions (CDFIs): A network of financial institutions that provide financing and other resources for underserved communities and small businesses. Website: cdfifund.gov

National Association of Development Companies (NADCO): An organization that provides resources and support for Certified Development Companies (CDCs) that provide financing and other resources for small businesses. Website: nadco.org

National Business Association (NBA): An organization that provides resources and support for small business owners and entrepreneurs. Website: nationalbusiness.org

Center for Women & Enterprise (CWE): CWE provides training, counseling, and resources to help women start and grow their businesses, including access to financing and networking opportunities. Website: cweonline.org

Minority Business Development Agency (MBDA): The MBDA provides resources and support to minority-owned businesses, including access to capital and business consulting services. Website: mbda.gov

Institute for Local Self-Reliance: The Institute for Local Self-Reliance is a nonprofit organization that provides research, resources, and support for local businesses and communities, including information on policies that support small businesses and sustainable development. Website: ilsr.org

Association for Enterprise Opportunity (AEO): AEO is a national membership organization that provides resources and support to microbusinesses and small businesses in underserved communities, including access to capital and technical assistance. Website: microenterpriseworks.org

Mack Graham

Informed Participation: 20 Civic Engagement Resources for Effective Advocacy

Rock the Vote: An organization focused on increasing youth voter participation through digital campaigns, grassroots organizing, and advocacy. Website: rockthevote.org

TurboVote: A tool for registering to vote and receiving election reminders. Website: turbovote.org

Vote.org: A tool for checking voter registration status, registering to vote, and finding polling locations. Website: vote.org

Ballotpedia: An online encyclopedia of American politics and elections that provides information on candidates and ballot measures. Website: ballotpedia.org/Main_Page

Run for Something: An organization focused on recruiting and supporting young progressives who want to run for local office. Website: runforsomething.net

Emily's List: An organization focused on electing pro-choice Democratic women to office. Website: emilyslist.org

National Democratic Training Committee: An organization that provides free online training resources for Democratic candidates and campaign staff. Website: traindemocrats.org

Latino Victory Fund: An organization focused on electing progressive Latino candidates to office. Website: latinovictory.us

New American Leaders: An organization focused on training and supporting immigrant candidates for public office. Website: newamericanleaders.org

The Center for Technology and Civic Life: An organization that provides tools and training for local election officials to improve the voting process. Website: techandciviclife.org

Project Vote Smart: A nonpartisan organization that provides information on candidates and elected officials, including their voting records and issue positions. Website: votesmart.org

League of Women Voters: An organization focused on promoting voter education and participation. Website: lwv.org

Fair Fight Action: An organization founded by Stacey Abrams to promote fair elections and voter participation. Website: fairfight.com

The Andrew Goodman Foundation: An organization focused on promoting youth voter participation and social justice. Website: andrewgoodman.org

Campaign Legal Center: An organization focused on protecting voting rights and fighting against gerrymandering. Website: campaignlegal.org

Indivisible: A network of local grassroots groups organizing for progressive policies and candidates. Website: indivisible.org

The Resistance Manual: An online resource for learning about and taking action on progressive issues. Website: resistancemanual.org

United We Dream: An organization that advocates for the rights of immigrant youth and their families. Website: unitedwedream.org

MoveOn.org: A platform for organizing and mobilizing on progressive issues. Website: front.moveon.org

Our Revolution: An organization founded by Bernie Sanders that promotes progressive policies and supports progressive candidates. Website: ourrevolution.com

<u>Neighborhood Hope Dealer:</u>
About the Author

Mack's journey to becoming a social justice advocate is a testament to the power of following your passions and finding purpose in your work. As a native New Yorker and a graduate of Stony Brook University, Mack began his career in the music industry in New York City. However, he soon realized that he yearned for a more meaningful career path that allowed him to give back to his community.

In 2010, Mack took a bold step and became a foster care planner, advocating for children and families in New York City and later in Austin, Texas. This experience proved to be transformative for Mack, igniting his passion for social services and advocating for underserved communities, particularly youth.

Over time, Mack's passion for social justice advocacy only grew stronger. He pursued a master's degree in Nonprofit Leadership from Fordham University, equipping him with the knowledge and skills necessary to understand the systemic issues that perpetuate inequality and promote community-led initiatives that create lasting change.

Mack's commitment to social justice advocacy is reflected in his extensive work with various organizations. He served as the Executive Director of the Long Beach Martin Luther King Center Director of Development at Newark Symphony Hall. In addition, he has been an active community organizer with the Gathering for Justice's rapid response task force – Justice League NYC, providing direct services and organizing in local and national communities.

Mack's most recent endeavor, founding Neighborhood Hope Dealerz, is a testament